Prophetic Anointing

Book 3 - The Prophetic Field Guide Series

Second Edition

Colette Toach

www.ami-bookshop.com

PROPHETIC ANOINTING
Book 3 - The Prophetic Field Guide Series
Second Edition

ISBN-10: 1626640947
ISBN-13: 978-1-62664-094-8

Copyright © 2015 by Apostolic Movement International, LLC
All rights reserved
5663 Balboa Ave #416,
San Diego,
California 92111,
United States of America

1st Printing June 2015
2nd Edition April 2016

Published by **Apostolic Movement International, LLC**
E-mail Address: admin@ami-bookshop.com
Web Address: www.ami-bookshop.com

All rights reserved under International Copyright Law.
Contents may not be reproduced in whole or in part in any form without the express written consent of the publisher.

Unless specified, all Scripture references taken from the New King James Version®. Copyright © 1982 by Thomas Nelson. Used by permission. All rights reserved..

Contents

- Contents 3
- Part 01 – The Prophetic Anointing 10
- Chapter 01 – The Prophetic Anointing Defined 16
  - Defining the Anointing 16
  - Tapping Into the Anointing 19
  - The Pearl of Great Value 25
- Chapter 02 – The External Anointing 30
  - The Anointing – the Most Basic Ingredient 31
  - Understanding the External Anointing 34
  - Experiencing The External Anointing 41
  - Ministries That Operate in The External Anointing . 43
- Chapter 03 – The Internal Anointing 46
  - The Promise - The Internal Anointing 46
  - Making the Anointing Comparison 50
- Chapter 04 – The Corporate Anointing 56
  - How the Prophet Brings Revival 58
  - When Should Revival Take Place? 64
  - Some Points on the Anointing 67
  - Come to Rest 72
- Part 02 – Prophetic Prayer and Intercession 74
  - Introduction to Prophetic Intercession 74
  - The 5 Functions of Prayer and Intercession 76

Chapter 05 – Prophetic Prayer 101 80
    Enter the Throne Room 84
    Set Aside the Weights 86
    Prayer vs. Intercession 89

Chapter 06 – Words of Power 96
    Why Words Count 96
    Your Activation Switch 98
    Intercession: Saying it Right 99
    Finding Your Words 103

Chapter 07 – The 1st Function of Prayer: Praise 108
    Prophetic Praise 109
    How to get Into His Throne Room 111

Chapter 08 – The 2nd Function: Petition 118
    Mastering Petitionary Prayer 118
    Rules of Engagement 120

Chapter 09 – The 3rd Function: Persistent Prayer 128
    The Fervent Prayer 129
    Move Past Your Plateau 130
    Persistent Prayer – Breaking Ground 134
    Breaking Ground 135

Chapter 10 – The 4th Function: Prophetic Warfare ... 140
    How to Engage in Prophetic Warfare 142
    Praying for Finances 146

Chapter 11 – The 5th Function: Prophetic Decree 158

Intercessor vs. Prophet	160
The Power of Prophetic Decree	161
Find Balance	172
Part 03 – Prophetic Music	**174**
Chapter 12 – The Origin of Music	178
Rocking With the 80's	179
We Are Not of This World	180
The Origin of Music	184
Chapter 13 – Finding The Right Frequency	190
The Power of Music	192
Music Opens a Door to the Spirit	193
Music Changes Creation	196
Chapter 14 – The Gentle Breeze of Jesus	200
The Gentle Breeze of Jesus	203
Touching People's Lives	205
The Price We Pay	208
Chapter 15 – Smashing Musical Mindsets	212
God Interferes	213
Understanding Musical Archetypes	216
Defining Musical Archetypes	218
Identifying Your Music Templates	220
Archetype Based on Country	222
Archetype Based on Programming	223
Break the Boundaries	224

Chapter 16 – Leading Worship Like a Prophet! 228
- A Truth to Remember 229
- The Internal Anointing 230
- How to Lead People Into the Presence of the Lord 232
- Worship is for the Church 238

Chapter 17 – The Prophet: Anointed to Worship......242
- "Bringing It" to the Baptists 243
- The Anointing Needs Focus..................................245
- Worship – A Two Way Street 249
- Time to Step Up! 252
- How to Receive a Double Portion of the Anointing 253

Chapter 18 – Identifying Prophetic Maturity 256
- God Working With Man 257
- God's Chasing You 258
- Signs of Prophetic Maturity..................................261
- Step Over the Threshold 275

About the Author 278

Recommendations by the Author 280
- Prophetic Boot Camp 280
- Prophetic Warfare..281
- Prophetic Functions 281
- Presentation of Prophecy.....................................282

Practical Prophetic Ministry 282
A.M.I. Prophetic School 283
Contact Information 284

PART 01

THE PROPHETIC ANOINTING

PART 01 – THE PROPHETIC ANOINTING

Without the anointing, you cannot fulfill the work that God has given you to do.

I do not think that any minister of the Word would disagree with me there. What you might not know, as one called as a prophet though, is that when the Lord called you to do His work, the anointing was part of the parcel that you received. Consider this passage:

> *Luke 4:18 The Spirit of the Lord is upon Me, because He has anointed Me to preach the gospel to the poor; he has sent Me to heal the brokenhearted, to proclaim liberty to the captives and recovery of sight to the blind, to set at liberty those who are oppressed,*

In other words, if the Lord has called you to do a work, He has given you the power that you need to fulfill it as well.

I see so many praying for the anointing, as if it is something that the Lord would deliberately withhold from you.

You need to change your thinking. The anointing and your calling are a complete package.

> **KEY PRINCIPLE**
>
> When the Lord called you, He gave you the anointing you needed to fulfill that call.

When this principle sinks in, you can spend less time asking God to anoint you, and more time asking how to walk in His anointing by faith.

Many have a strange idea about the anointing though. They think of it as something that comes and goes. You imagine that the Lord anoints you just once, but then you must qualify for it again, and again.

Well, to a certain extent, that was true in days gone by. Before Christ came - that is exactly what it was like when you needed the anointing. The Holy Spirit descended on a great man of faith, and then left him once the work was done.

Samson was a great example of this. The anointing would come upon him suddenly, and when that happened, he accomplished incredible feats. Once the anointing left him though, he was weak once again.

That is because Jesus had not yet died for our sins! Man was contaminated through sin. They had to sacrifice often to atone and "cover over" the sin in their lives. And so a very righteous God could not reside with a very sinful man.

I often wonder to myself how hard it must have been in those days. They had to keep the law using their will alone. They did not have the Holy Spirit within to make right choices. They had to wait for God to "come upon them" before they felt Him.

No wonder the coming of Christ was such a mind-blowing change of thinking for the Early Church. For the first time, the anointing came... and remained!

> *1 John 2:27 But the anointing which you have received from Him abides in you, and you do not need that anyone teach you; but as the same anointing teaches you concerning all things, and is true, and is not a lie, and just as it has taught you, you will abide in Him.*

I love this passage. John tells us here, that the anointing that they received did not leave! It did not "come upon" and then "lift" from them again, and again.

Instead of having to push through with pure willpower, they had a "big brother" in their corner by the name of the Holy Spirit.

For the first time ever, a righteous God could dwell within a sinful man – all because of the blood of Christ that washes away our sin.

When you understand this concept, you will not ask God again to "give you the anointing again" but you will ask Him to increase what you already have. You will ask Him for wisdom to use what is already in your spirit.

Then just as this scripture above says, that very anointing will teach you what you need to do to fulfill your purpose.

In the next couple of chapters we are going to look at the New Testament prophet. For it is the anointing that differentiates the Old from the New Testament prophet quite considerably.

In the Old Testament, the prophet had to wait for God to suddenly come upon him before he could speak. The same is not true of the New Testament prophet.

Instead, when God calls and anoints you, He deposits that anointing right inside of your spirit. That means you carry it with you everywhere you go.

Now that does not mean that it is "your" anointing. It simply means that you have a reserve of power in your spirit that the Holy Spirit can use when He pleases. He does not need to wait for you to be "righteous" according to the flesh, but He just needs to wait until you are available.

Keep these simple principles in mind as we look in greater detail at what we now have in Christ. You will learn that not only do we still have the external anointing just like they had in the Old Testament, but that we now have the internal anointing, which is depicted as streams of living water.

This anointing is what sets you apart as a prophet. So let's teach you to tap into it, so that you can gush over the Church and bring it to life!

CHAPTER 01

THE PROPHETIC ANOINTING DEFINED

Chapter 01 – The Prophetic Anointing Defined

The first thing you need to know is that you already have the prophetic anointing. If God has called you to the prophetic ministry, you already have within you the anointing to get the job done.

That is the easy part. You know, so many people are confused. They think that they have to hop from conference to conference to get the prophetic anointing. No, you already have it. The part that is difficult is learning to identify it and then to flow in it correctly.

Defining the Anointing

> *John 7:38 He who believes in Me, as the Scripture has said, out of his heart will flow rivers of living water.*

As a child I was really blessed. I grew up living near many recreational parks. My father, quite the adventurer, loved to take us out on weekends to visit these parks.

There was one in particular that he liked to take us to. With its rolling hills, it was the perfect place for some time alone. The best part of all though, was the meandering river that cut through the hills from one end to the other.

We would head out early, and spread our blanket out on the soft, fragrant grass. A picnic would follow with lots of goodies. After we were done, we would pack up, put all our stuff back in the car, and then we would go walking.

THE BUBBLING BROOK

We would find the river and follow it as much as we could. We would explore and see what there was to find: trees, stones, hidden ditches or bridges. It was fun to seek out the perfect skipping stone to send skimming over the water.

Even though this was years ago, just speaking about it, I can smell the fresh soil and the plant life next to the river. I can hear the sound of the water making a gentle chuckle as it flows over the rocks.

It is as real to me as if I went there yesterday. Each time I bring this memory to mind, it brings with it that familiar feeling of peace.

The picture I painted is the perfect illustration of the prophetic anointing. It is like a gentle, bubbling brook that brings peace, joy and rest. It is not a mighty waterfall that comes splashing, picking you up and tossing you around. No, that is the external anointing and that comes by the will of God alone.

The prophetic anointing is something entirely different. It is a gentle bubbling that originates from deep within you. If you would just stop for a moment, you would come to realize that you have been experiencing this for some time.

Perhaps you have been comparing yourself to other ministers and feeling a little insecure.

The Mighty Waterfall – The External Anointing

You look at all these big revivalists and they bring a mighty outpouring of the Spirit. People talk about the "fire" and the "water," and people are getting slain in the spirit in their meetings. You see healings, miracles, shakings and a whole bunch of other stuff going on.

You take a step back and think, "Wow!"

You compare yourself to them and when you look inside, you think, "Here I stand with just my little bubbling brook."

You know, I had the opportunity to go to the Rheinfall in Switzerland. It is the largest waterfall in Europe. It is absolutely magnificent. The sound of the water is so loud that you have to shout at one another to be heard.

It roars in your ears. A fine mist covers the whole river because of the intensity at which the water hits the lake with below. It is incredible.

I have been there a few times to visit, and each time has been wonderful, but I didn't spend hours there. You can only spend so long staring at a waterfall, and well... you have seen a waterfall. It is wonderful, it is magnificent and I take the experience home with me, but it is a place I have visited as a tourist only once or twice.

WATERFALL VS. BROOK

By comparison, as a child, when we went to the bubbling brook, I could sit there for hours just quietly taking in the sounds and smells. That sound refreshed my spirit. I could go back again, and again and never grow weary of it.

It is great to have the great outpourings. We need them to be refreshed from time to time, but you can't live there.

TAPPING INTO THE ANOINTING

What you have is an anointing that people can take home with them. That when touched by it, continues to work within them. It is the kind of anointing that I spoke about in the introduction from 1 John 2:27. It is an anointing that abides.

You don't take a bucket of water and splash the water on their heads. Rather you are releasing a bubbling brook into their spirits. You will bring the spirit inside of them to life! It is an anointing that will continue to bubble and flow like a beautiful spring that will come up and feed them again and again.

What It Feels Like

So when you experience the anointing, realize that it is going to bubble from deep inside. I feel it right in the pit of my stomach. I feel it sometimes like butterflies. It is like the feeling you get the night before Christmas when you were hoping to get that "special something." You lay in bed at night and you were so excited. Your stomach did flips and you couldn't sleep - you couldn't eat. Well, that's how I felt the night before I got married. I couldn't sleep the whole night. I was so excited and terrified all at the same time.

That is what the internal anointing feels like. Now the first time that you experience it, it is probably going to be pretty strong. Yes, there are many different manifestations of the anointing, but I am just just covering the prophetic anointing here.

It may start very strong at the beginning, or perhaps very gentle. It will nudge you from deep within saying, "Hello, remember me? I am here, I want to tell you something." That's the Holy Spirit speaking inside of you.

How to Identify It

To hear that gentle voice you need to shut up. I know that you hear me telling you to do that a lot, but by the end of this series you will be used to me saying it. That is because as prophets, we either do not know how, or find it really hard to sit quietly instead of shouting our mouths off.

> **KEY PRINCIPLE**
>
> You need to learn to be quiet long enough to hear the voice of the Lord within.

You will feel this anointing as a gentle stirring. The Holy Spirit is not going to run up to you, slap you on the side of the head and say, "Prophesy."

It doesn't happen that way. He is going to gently remind you, and that reminder is going to come from deep down inside. You are not living in Old Testament times when the Lord had to wait for you to be righteous before He could come upon you. Now He can speak to you from within your spirit any time that He pleases. Your part in this conversation is to be silent long enough to hear Him.

HOW TO TAP INTO THE ANOINTING

How are you going to tap into it? We know we have this river of living water inside of us, and sometimes you even feel it. Now, what do you do with it?

You need to realize that releasing this anointing is very much the same as journaling. I have already taken you through the whole process of decreeing, and journaling in *The Prophetic Functions* book. I will also teach you about intercession later on in this book.

So, by now you should be familiar with the stirring you feel inside your belly. When you start to journal it feels slow, but the more you write, the easier it gets. The anointing starts to flow and the words flow faster than you can type - faster than you can speak. You feel that bubbling coming up inside of you.

Well, that is the prophetic anointing that you have been experiencing! You have been experiencing it all along. Now you need to learn to use it when ministering.

1. MAKE YOURSELF AVAILABLE

The first thing you need to do is make yourself available. Say now, you are in a meeting, or somebody comes to you for prayer. You can only say, "Lord, I am a vessel. I have got your living waters inside of me. I open up my mouth and it is for you to fill it."

> **KEY PRINCIPLE**
>
> You tap into the anointing by making yourself available, desiring to be used by the Lord, and by stepping out in faith.

2. FAITH IS THE KEY

You can learn to flow in the spirit this way. Once you identify the river of living water inside of you, you can trigger it by faith at any time. If I make a conscious effort to stop and tap into the anointing, I can release that anointing any time I desire, because I am a prophet.

Now keep in mind that I am speaking about the anointing here, and not the gifts of the Spirit! The gifts are only manifested by the Holy Spirit. However, when those gifts do manifest, if you act in faith, the anointing will follow.

> **KEY PRINCIPLE**
>
> The gifts: manifested as the Holy Spirit wills.
>
> The anointing that brings the revelation to pass: released by your faith.

When you reach prophetic office, you are going to realize that the anointing is available to you at any time.

3. IT REMAINS IN YOUR SPIRIT.

There are times though when people come to you and you need to tap into that anointing fast.

People sometimes need ministry at the most inconvenient times! The doorbell rings, and you just had a fight with your spouse, the house is a mess, you messed up at work that day, you stubbed your toe, and then tripped over the dog on your way to answer the door.

There, standing in front of you, is someone saying, "Please could you pray for me?"

With an incredulous intake of breath, you think, "Are you kidding me, Lord? The last thing I feel right now is your power. I had a horrible day, and I don't feel very spiritual at all at the moment."

Well then, just as well, the anointing is not dependent on you, hey? Thank goodness it depends on the Holy Spirit.

The "Emergency" Situation

Ok, so when faced with such a situation, this is what you want to do.

The first thing you want to do is to have a cup of coffee (unless you are one of those tea drinkers). Chill out, calm down, take a deep breath, and make yourself available to the Lord.

"You alone know Father, that if this depends on me, I am going to end up depressing this person instead of ministering to them. But, here I am, Lord. I make myself available to you."

When you do that, you will feel peace come into your spirit. Maybe you will get revelation, and maybe you won't, but the point is that you can stop and tap into the anointing. You can still pray in faith and expect the Holy Spirit to show up.

If that person comes to you with a need, and you don't get revelation, you can still tap into the anointing and say, "Father, I bring this need to you and I stand against this attack right now in the name of Jesus. I speak your blessing on their circumstances. Satan, I don't care where you got in, you loose your hold!"

You can't help but feel the anointing. You can't help but tap into it.

THE PEARL OF GREAT VALUE

Let go of all these pictures of grandeur that are based on what you have seen others do. Prophets have let go of this treasure - their little, bubbling brook. They desire so much to flow in the signs and wonders that they see in healing revivalists. They seek what everyone else has, and in so doing, they let go of this precious pearl.

This anointing is like the pearl spoken of in Matthew 13:46. In this parable, the merchant sold everything so that he could get hold of a pearl of great value.

You have let go of this beautiful pearl to try to have all the "great things" out there.

You see evangelists everywhere, and everybody runs from one revival to the next because they all eventually fizzle down. The thing is, the prophetic anointing never fizzles down. It only grows stronger, and deeper, and it lasts. If you can tap into it and speak into the lives of God's people, the change will last. It can be available to you any time, 24 hours a day.

Don't let go of this treasure because you want to be like everybody else. Well, maybe it is just the rebel in me, but I don't want to be like everybody else. I want to be a prophet and I want to stand up as a prophet, in the power of God.

A Sign and a Wonder

I want to release change into the hearts of God's people. I want to ignite you. I want to inspire you.

Now tell me that this is not a sign and a wonder! Tell me, if you speak healing into the life of someone, and they go away having experienced Jesus, is that not a sign and a wonder?

What are the turning points of your Christian life? Are they not the experiences that you had with the Lord? Those convictions, rhema words and the times with Him that transformed the way you saw things?

Those are signs and wonders! It is no less miraculous than a physical healing, or an external manifestation of the anointing.

Don't let go of the pearl you have, for anything! Grasp it and develop it, and rise up in it. Be proud of it, because it is what God has given you.

It is – the prophetic anointing!

> **KEY PRINCIPLE**
>
> Without the anointing, you are nothing. You are just somebody who flows in a couple of prophetic gifts.

Be the prophet that God has called you to be, and tap into this treasure.

Take hold of that anointing and use it in every part of your life. You are going to see dramatic change in your life and in the lives of others.

CHAPTER 02

THE EXTERNAL ANOINTING

Chapter 02 – The External Anointing

Acts 2:3 Then there appeared to them divided tongues, as of fire, and one sat upon each of them.

I love to cook. I cook quite often, but you know, even somebody like myself who is used to cooking, has bad days.

There has even been the odd occasion when passionate cooking turned into a definite disaster!

You see, I love to collect spices of different kinds. I remember that I had an awesome collection of Indian spices. I was going to make the most divine curry you ever tasted!

So, I added cardamom, garam masala, curry powder, crushed coriander, anise, and for good measure, enough garlic and ginger to give it a "zing." I thought that this was going to be my shining moment.

I mixed everything together, and let it stew for a nice long time. As it was simmering, it smelled so good! Before long, the meat was ready. I hungrily took a big mouthful and… it was awful.

Do you know why it was awful? It all fell apart because I forgot to add the salt! I was so busy with all the new spices that I had found at a local Indian store that I forgot the most important ingredient of all - simple, boring salt.

You know, the crazy thing is, you can put in all the most exotic, aromatic spices in the world, but if you leave out salt, the most basic, boring, easy-to-find, everywhere spice - your food tastes horrible.

THE ANOINTING – THE MOST BASIC INGREDIENT

It is the same mistake that so many people make when it comes to ministry. They flow in "this" and in "that" gift, and they know "this" principle and "that" principle. They know how to stand, how to speak, and they know how to dress, impress, and pray up a storm.

Unfortunately though, in amongst doing "the stuff," they leave out salt – which is the anointing.

It says in Matthew 5:13:

> *You are the salt of the earth; but if the salt loses its flavor, how shall it be seasoned? It is then good for nothing but to be thrown out and trampled underfoot by men.*

See, that was the state of my poor curry. All that work and all that effort for this beautiful curry dish that nobody could eat until I salted it.

Just a bit of salt, and the curry was transformed into something spectacular.

You can have all the gifts. You can have all the skills. You can preach well, speak well, and stand well.

> **KEY PRINCIPLE**
>
> Without the anointing, you are an unsalted, tasteless, and boring food. You are food that will not leave an impression. A ministry that will not bring change.

YOU NEED THE ANOINTING

In the previous chapter, we already looked at the prophetic anointing. For the next two chapters, I am going to compare the internal prophetic anointing with the external anointing, so you can learn to identify the difference between the two.

Everybody wants the fancy spices. Everyone wants the cardamom, garam masala and coriander. They are like the great outpourings that stir my emotions and get me fired up and inspired!

Then I go home, and what feeds me? Where is the salt? Where is the boring day-to-day stuff that keeps us alive? The anointing of God is not just a once-in-a-day, or once-in-a-lifetime, experience. It is something that we should live with all the time. It is something that you should be releasing into the Body of Christ all of the time.

MOVING FROM EXTERNAL TO INTERNAL

So first, let's have a look at the differences between the internal and the external anointing, and how it relates to you as a prophet.

I am going to explain a bit more from my own experience concerning these two categories of anointing.

> **Just a word before we begin:** It is very likely that before you entered into prophetic training, that you were more familiar with the external anointing.

In fact, it is quite common for those who had an evangelistic ministry before to then move into the prophetic.

Now if you are not familiar with the two types of anointing, it could scare you a bit. The reason being - from experiencing external outpourings, everything changes and slows down with the internal.

Where before everything was so strong, powerful and clear, you now feel like the anointing has left you entirely.

You think, "Okay, why am I not getting these loud words of wisdom? Why am I not getting these clear revelations like I did before?"

Chill out, you are just moving in the prophetic. It is no less clear - it is just a lot different. The revelation is still coming. You just need to learn to identify it.

Understanding the External Anointing

As I discussed in our last chapter, you have the internal anointing on tap. I love it. You know, the Lord was gracious to me. He let me go through the prophetic first, and led me through the evangelistic, afterwards.

You know what a death that was? Yes, it was a death because I was so used to relying on the internal anointing. When the Lord stopped that, and made me rely only on the external, I thought I would literally die. I was used to, "Okay, let's pray." The anointing would flow, and I could pour out.

1. Comes by God's Will Alone

Then, when the external anointing came, I realized that it comes only by the will of God. The evangelistic training was the most intense, devastating experience of my life because I came to realize that without the external anointing, I was nothing.

I was 100% dependent on that external anointing, and when it wasn't there, I was really just a filthy, rotten sinner that had nothing to offer anybody.

Good training. Tough training… but I like being a prophet a lot better.

As a prophet, when you need to pray or need revelation, you can submit yourself to the Lord and get it immediately. You learn to tap into it. So this is one of the main differences.

You can speak in tongues at any time, can't you? You can tap into the internal anointing at any time, but the external anointing comes by the will of God. It's by His timing, and it is entirely dependent on when He wants to release it.

2. Old Testament vs. New Testament

Another difference, is that the internal anointing was not available to the Old Testament saints. Did you know that? They didn't have the rivers of living waters that dwell within you. You never read of rivers of living water available in the Old Testament. They only had the external anointing.

Here is a list of some great heroes of old. Each one of these operated powerfully in the anointing, yet still not having the fullness of what we have today!

> *Hebrews 11:32 And what more shall I say? For the time would fail me to tell of Gideon and Barak and Samson and Jephthah, also of David and Samuel and the prophets: 33 who through faith subdued kingdoms, worked righteousness, obtained promises, stopped the mouths of lions, 34 quenched the violence of fire, escaped the edge of the sword, out of weakness were made*

> strong, became valiant in battle, turned to flight the armies of the aliens.

I want you to pay special attention to something you will read a lot of regarding the anointing.

> *Judges 6:34 But the Spirit of the Lord came upon Gideon; then he blew the trumpet, and the Abiezrites gathered behind him.*

"When the Holy Spirit came upon… " You will see this phrase repeated throughout Scripture.

KEY PRINCIPLE

> In the Old Testament, the anointing came upon them from without. In the New Testament, we have the anointing that rises up from within.

Samson, for example, became strong when the anointing came upon him. He might have been able to carry a city gate up a mountain, however he did not have the spirit within to give him the confirmation, or warning he needed to stay away from Delilah! Sure, he experienced the anointing from without, but it wasn't inside of him. He couldn't tap into it any time he wanted to.

Every time he displayed his strength, do you notice that the Word says, "The spirit of the Lord came upon him"?

David said, "By my God, I can leap over a wall." The spirit of God had to come upon him.

It was the same with the prophets. The anointing had to come upon them. Things changed when the New Testament came along.

Suddenly, we have something that the Old Testament saints didn't have. We have the Holy Spirit dwelling within us.

3. What was New in the New Testament

We have something else they also did not have in the Old Testament. It is found in this little passage,

> *Mark 16:17 And these signs will follow those who believe: In My name they will cast out demons; they will speak with new tongues.*

You do not find any of the Old Testament saints speaking in tongues! In the New Testament, man enters into a brand new relationship with the Holy Spirit.

Because of what Jesus did, He could take our sins to the Father. We could be washed clean of sin. From that moment onwards, a very righteous God could come and dwell within very sinful man.

In the Old Testament, this wasn't possible. God could not coexist with sinful man. When Adam and Eve sinned, God had to remove them from the Garden of Eden. He couldn't have that intimate relationship with them anymore because they had opened the door to sin.

From that moment onwards, He started preparing the way for Jesus to come.

THE DIFFERENCE JESUS MADE

When Jesus died, He enabled us to receive the Holy Spirit and have Him dwell within us. You did not need to hope and pray any more that the Lord would "suddenly" come upon you.

No longer do we have to wait for God to speak. For the first time, we could have God living inside of us, and dwelling within our spirits.

4. AVAILABLE TO EVERY SAINT

The other difference is that the internal anointing is available to all believers, whereas in the Old Testament, the Lord was selective with whom He poured His spirit out on.

He didn't just anoint whom He wanted. Look at Saul for example. The Holy Spirit came upon him when He wanted to, but also left him when He wanted to. When the Spirit left Saul, there was no going back for him.

Even though he tried so hard to get it back – he needed David to come and play the harp for him to experience some anointing again.

Well, praise the Lord, that in today's day and age, the anointing never leaves us no matter how much we sin and fail.

> **KEY PRINCIPLE**
>
> No matter how much you mess up, no matter how many mistakes you have made, the anointing of God stays with you and remains with you always.

GOD IS NO LONGER SELECTIVE

For some reason, many believers haven't got this concept yet. They still think that they have to work and strive for the anointing. "You have to be a better prophet, or you have to be a more righteous minister." No, the anointing is within you.

Sure, what you do may hinder the anointing from flowing out, but your sin doesn't take it away.

In the New Testament, we have a terrific gift of the anointing that stays with us no matter how much we fail - no matter how much we mess up. The anointing is in your spirit and the Lord is not going to reject you.

It means, that if you swore to that driver on the way home from work yesterday, (okay, you should probably work on that) it doesn't mean that you have lost your prophetic anointing!

As believers, this anointing is always available to us. No matter what you do, no matter how much you fail, the Holy Spirit remains. The rivers of living water may be plugged up from time to time by your silly mistakes, but it doesn't leave. You just need to learn to stir it up again.

5. Holiness vs. Faith

You receive the anointing through faith, but in the Old Testament, they received it by holiness. This is another wonderful difference between the Old and the New Testament. They experienced it through righteousness and holy living.

Look at what happened to Saul and King Solomon. Solomon was so anointed that when he dedicated the temple, the power of God came down strongly, to the extent that the priests couldn't stand to minister.

It didn't stay that way though. When he sinned and failed, the anointing left. The Lord had to remove Himself from him.

We see it again, and again through the Scriptures. The anointing would come upon somebody, but when they failed, it had to leave them again.

ANOINTED SINNERS?!

In the New Testament, we receive the anointing by faith. Hasn't it bothered you sometimes, when you see people that you know are not in right standing before God, but yet still minister with a powerful anointing?

When I look at some of the revivalists of old, I think, "Wow, some of them had some serious issues and even some weirder doctrines."

Yet, despite their deception - miracles still occurred! Why?

Because the anointing is received by faith and not by righteousness. In fact, I would daresay that faith is righteousness, because faith is based on how holy the blood of Jesus is and not how holy we are!

Because of what Jesus did on the cross, we are righteous in the sight of God! Now that is something to get excited about!

I will keep on discussing the difference between the external and internal anointing in the next chapter, but for now, I want to speak briefly on what experiencing the external anointing is like.

EXPERIENCING THE EXTERNAL ANOINTING

> *2 Chronicles 5:14 So that the priests could not continue ministering because of the cloud; for the glory of the Lord filled the house of God.*

The most outstanding effect that the external anointing has on you is a physical one. In this passage, we see something taking place that is also common in today's church. When the anointing came, people had a hard time standing up!

1. Feels Like a Rainstorm

It is like standing under a rainstorm that sweeps you away! It comes upon you, and you will feel it like Aaron did when he was anointed and the oil dripped from his head down to his toes.

You might feel a warm feeling flow over you, or a physical weakness in His presence. There is no doubt when the external anointing is there – you will feel it coming upon you externally, and physically.

2. Demons Manifest

Another common experience in revival meetings, is the manifestation of demons. Follow Jesus' ministry, and you will see that there was no shortage of demons manifesting all over the place!

Now a lot of people get confused about this. They sometimes confuse demon manifestations with a work of the Holy Spirit – not realizing that the demon is manifesting because of the presence of the Holy Spirit!

Just like the priests could not stand to minister, so also will demons manifest in the external glory of God. This is certainly what happened to Saul when David was playing his harp, and a demonic force overcame Saul. The result? Spears were hurled and David had to run for cover. Now wouldn't it have been nice if David could have just rebuked that demon? Unfortunately, Jesus had not yet come.

3. Physical Empowerment

The external anointing gives physical strength and power – just like it did for Samson. He had the strength to kill hundreds of men with the jawbone of a donkey. Unfortunately, after the anointing lifted, he was weak once again!

Gideon was given supernatural boldness, Elijah outran a chariot, and David was known to jump over a wall. The physical effect of this anointing is what makes it stand out the most.

Ministries That Operate In The External Anointing

While the prophet might be used of God to operate in this anointing every now and again, it is most often seen in the evangelistic and apostolic ministries.

I do not think I will get a lot of argument on that. You only need to look at the Church today to see the Lord move in this way amongst revivalists.

If you consider that the role of the evangelist is to bring the Good News, you see why the external anointing is needed. When you see how the apostle has to lay a new foundation for the Church, you realize that it is going to take supernatural wisdom to bring that about.

THE PROPHET AND THE ANOINTING

If you consider that the call of the prophet is to see in the spirit and to set God's people in place, you will understand why you flow more in the internal anointing. The Lord has given you oil that heals the heart of man.

He has given you wisdom to set believers in place, and the anointing to draw them closer to Jesus. The last thing you want when ushering people into the secret place with Jesus is a violent demon manifestation!

The kind of anointing you flow in will draw people into a face-to-face relationship with Jesus. Deliverance will come naturally as you take them through this process. I like to say that we "displace" the demons when we bring people closer to Jesus!

Let the evangelists do their job and flow in the external anointing. Let them set the Church on fire and draw in unbelievers. You do your job by helping believers find a place and so they can reach maturity!

Together, we are a body. Together we will equip the people of God to do good works of every kind!

CHAPTER 03

THE INTERNAL ANOINTING

Chapter 03 – The Internal Anointing

> *John 20:22 And when He had said this, He breathed on them, and said to them, "Receive the Holy Spirit,..."*

> *Hebrews 11:13 These all died in faith, not having received the promises, but having seen them afar off were assured of them, embraced them and confessed that they were strangers and pilgrims on the earth.*

I imagined how it must have been for Abraham, knowing what was to come, but never getting to see it. From the time that he offered Isaac on that altar, he knew that he had just opened a new door in the spirit.

One that he would never get to see with his natural eyes.

It says in Hebrews 11:13, that all these great men of faith died seeing the promise that was to come, but never having experienced it for themselves.

The Promise - The Internal Anointing

What was "the promise" exactly? Well that is what we have been discussing in the last few chapters.

> *Ezekiel 36:27 I will put My Spirit within you and cause you to walk in My statutes, and you will keep My judgments and do them*

This is the indwelling of the Holy Spirit. It is the ability to flow outwards from the rivers within. To speak in tongues, prophesy, and have the Lord right there in every moment of your day.

We have so much more in the New Testament. If you can take hold of this promise, you will also flow in the anointing God set aside for you as a prophet!

In the Old Testament they were given a set of rules that they had to strictly obey. If they did not, they were cursed. What a stark contrast this scripture is in light of that:

> *Romans 8:4 that the righteous requirement of the law might be fulfilled in us who do not walk according to the flesh but according to the Spirit.*

No longer were God's people told to just "obey," but they were now given the ability to follow each commandment. They were now told to "walk in the spirit!"

1. YOU CAN WALK IN THE SPIRIT

While the external anointing was dependent on your righteousness, in the New Testament, we can choose to walk in the spirit. Go and read Romans (one of my favorite books of the Bible) where Paul speaks repeatedly of not fulfilling the lusts of the flesh, but to rather walk in the spirit.

They couldn't do that in the Old Testament. They only had the law. The lines were very clear: there was right and wrong, and they could choose to sin, or not to sin.

Of course, it did not help at all that they had the seed of sin, so they kept messing up. They kept sinning, and God had to punish them - then they came running back to Him again. It was a crazy dance that repeated itself from one generation to the next.

In the New Testament though, we don't have that problem. We can choose to walk in the spirit. Romans 8:4 says that when you walk in the spirit, you do not fulfill the lusts of the flesh.

No longer is it a case of, "I must not sin. I must not sin. I must not sin." It is now a case of, "I must walk in the spirit and I must walk in right standing with God."

By walking in the spirit, we naturally don't fulfill the lusts of the flesh. Yes, we still mess up. We are human. We fail and we sin.

Apostle Paul says, "Oh, wretched man that I am. Who will deliver me from this body of flesh?" I am sure that we have all had moments in our lives when we thought, "Okay Lord, I think that I am never going to get it right."

> **KEY PRINCIPLE**
>
> We can choose to walk in the spirit. This is a choice that they didn't have in the Old Testament.

They didn't have the Holy Spirit inside of them to help them to walk in the spirit, so that they did not fulfill the lusts of the flesh.

2. The Anointing Remains

You can feel the internal anointing through the gift of discerning of spirits. This really, is what I have experienced in my own life. You can feel it on materials and teachings. You can pick up a book from somebody that is flowing in the internal anointing, and you can sense the anointing on it.

The external anointing is a bit different. It is like a rhema word that comes for a specific moment in time. It comes and it leaves.

This is not true of the internal anointing. If I recorded a meeting when I flowed in the internal anointing, you will experience that same anointing each time you listen, or watch it.

With the external anointing, what might have felt anointed in a meeting, will seem to lose its power when you listen to the message later on. Why? It is because the anointing came down for a specific purpose and message. It was a kairos time for you.

So don't be confused if you experienced something while watching a particular message, to never experience that same power again.

Perhaps the first time you might have experienced the power of God. Then, the next time you listened to that message, you did not feel a thing. Why? Well, that's the difference between the internal and the external anointing.

The internal you can feel again, and again, whereas the external is just for the moment. It comes, and then it is gone.

MAKING THE ANOINTING COMPARISON

How do these two types of anointing relate to the prophet? The prophet functions primarily in the internal anointing, as does the teacher. The evangelist, however, tends to function in the external. The pastor can do a little bit of both. That is a fivefold ministry lesson, and I am not going to get into that right here.

As a prophet, you will experience the external anointing at times. I experience it more when I speak a decree or release someone prophetically, into a ministry office.

I have come to realize that this anointing comes because God is doing a work in the person I am ministering to. This isn't something I am imparting or releasing, but this is something that the Holy Spirit is doing.

When I release somebody into office or into training, sometimes I don't feel anything on the inside. The anointing comes from without. When I feel this, then I know the Holy Spirit is doing something in that person.

I believe that I experience this when I am releasing somebody into a ministry office, because the Holy Spirit is giving them the authority, and not me!

I can't give them the authority. I can just be used of God to speak the decree. I can open my big mouth (I am really good at that) and release what I need to release. I can't anoint them - it is the Holy Spirit that anoints, not me. It is the Holy Spirit that convicts, not me. I can just be a vessel.

INTERNAL ANOINTING: INNER HEALING

For general prophetic words and inner healing, you will experience more of the internal anointing. When you feel it, it may start in your stomach. You might feel warm or you may feel like oil is being poured over you.

It is gentle and soothing. This anointing is like a bubbling brook - remember? You are going to feel that "bubbling up" especially when you minister inner healing.

When you learn to tap into that anointing, you can release it when you write a letter, or if you write a book. Pick up *Practical Prophetic Ministry* and tell me if it doesn't call you to death within the first two pages!

There is an anointing in there, and it works for every prophet that reads it. I have yet to find somebody who has a real call who hasn't experienced something when reading that book.

It is the same with the *Dreams and Visions* book. Why? When I wrote it, I wrote it with the anointing. You can do it too. You can learn to tap into your spirit and write with the anointing.

Stop trying to write with your head. Learn to tap into your spirit. Go and edit it later, but release what's in your spirit first. Once you have released what's in your spirit, you can go and do the analytical thing afterwards, but let's tap into the anointing first.

Again, do you realize the treasure that you have? You have this bubbling brook deep within. Yes, there will be times when you will experience the external anointing, and there will be times when you will release a word of God, or you will feel the Holy Spirit move on that person. These are exciting times, but you don't live there as a prophet.

Those are great times, but the best times are when you lay your hands on somebody, and you feel that bubbling inside. The best times are when you speak healing to their hearts and you see change in their lives.

ALL WE NEED - JESUS

How can we walk around and call ourselves Christians and not know Christ? The Church out there is dead. It is a Church that is looking for all the candy, but doesn't know the salt of Christ.

They do not know His touch and the reality of who He is. They don't know His sense of humor. They don't know Him face-to-face. When they have struggles, they have to go to the nearest prophet.

> *KEY PRINCIPLE*
>
> Your mandate as a prophet is to introduce Jesus to His people, but it is only going to happen with the anointing.

So you need to learn to tap into the anointing. You need to learn to release it. When you start experiencing change in the lives of God's people, no death you went through, no struggle, and no rejection, will matter anymore.

The pure joy of being used by the Lord, to experience Him, and to have other people experience Him, defines us. It is what sets us apart, and what makes this walk something incredible.

CHAPTER 04

THE CORPORATE ANOINTING

Chapter 04 – The Corporate Anointing

> *Matthew 18:20 For where two or three are gathered together in My name, I am there in the midst of them.*

When was the last time your church prayer meeting caused an earthquake? Well that was certainly a common event in the New Testament Church! When the church got together to pray, Peter was let out of prison, Paul and Silas dismantled prison bars, and the ground shook.

If two could chase ten thousand in the Old Testament, how much more in the New? I love how the Lord has joined us as a body. We have the Spirit that raised Jesus from the dead inside of us.

We have the authority within our spirits to cast a mountain into the sea. However, when we come together, something amazing happens. All of that potential is joined to your brothers and sisters, and that anointing is amplified.

You see, when we get together and add all our little "streams" together, we cause the external anointing to come.

Do you see the passage above in Matthew 18:20? It says that when two or three are gathered (in unity), that the Holy Spirit will show up!

THE SECRET TO REVIVAL

There are many seeking the Lord for the secret to revival. Many pin it on a great man or woman of God. However, each time a revival took place, you can be sure that it was the result of the hungry hearts of God's people crying out for His power.

You can be sure it was when two or three gathered in His name and joined their hearts together, that caused the rain to fall.

Now as a prophet, you already know that you are meant to bring the Church into unity.

So in this chapter, I want to look at why this is so important. Perhaps you do not realize that you hold the secret to bringing revival to the Church!

You will not bring it about by standing out front and giving prophetic words. It will not happen even if you heal a few sick people or preach a fiery sermon.

> **KEY PRINCIPLE**
>
> You are going to accomplish revival by joining the hearts of God's people together.

It is your job to bring the Church into unity – to gather the "two or three" so that the external anointing can come in power!

HOW THE PROPHET BRINGS REVIVAL

It was when the Disciples were gathered in the upper room that the tongues of fire fell and they were filled with power. If we are to see the kind of power that we need in the Church to bring real change, we need this kind of unity again.

When God's people get together and pray in faith, God always answers. The problem here does not lie with the Lord, but with getting His people together to pray in faith. When the Israelites cried out with one voice for a deliverer, the Lord sent Moses.

When Esther and Mordecai prayed for salvation, God gave them favor. When Solomon and the people prayed before God at the dedication of the temple, the anointing came down so strongly that the priests could not stand to minister.

Incredible things happen when our hearts are knit as one. The first thing that the prophet can do to bring about this kind of unity is by getting off the pulpit and pointing God's people to Jesus!

1. GET 'EM HOOKED UP TO JESUS

We have spoken long and hard in this series about the purpose of a prophet. You know you are called to point people to the Lord.

When this happens though, something incredible will take place. When we all "hook up" to Jesus, we will suddenly find ourselves in unity.

You are not going to get the Church into unity by trying to get them to agree on doctrine.

You are also not going to get the Church into unity by getting them to believe your prophetic word.

> **KEY PRINCIPLE**
>
> The only way we will get into unity is when we share the same spirit – the spirit of Christ! When everyone has a relationship with Jesus, the rest is easy.

When the Church taps into Jesus, they tap into unity. Once they tap into unity - revival will follow. If we, as prophets, accomplish nothing else but bring every believer into a face-to-face relationship with Jesus, we have accomplished the bulk of what God has put us on this earth to do.

2. Remove Veils

The greatest hindrance to unity is the veils that separate us from the Lord and one another. As a prophet, you will need to help expose these veils.

Each veil has a different name depending on the person. There are some who are covered over with veils of bitterness and fear. Others hide behind guilt and condemnation.

Each veil found its place through bad experiences of the past. They were put there by bad decisions and responses to those experiences.

> **KEY PRINCIPLE**
>
> The moment the Holy Spirit starts to draw us into unity, you can be sure that a time of fire is coming!

Before Joshua could lead the children of Israel across the Jordan, they had a day of foreskin chopping - not a pretty picture.

Before the promise could come to pass, they had to remove the veils – the things that stood in the way of their covenant with the Lord.

HINDRANCE TO THE ANOINTING

The same holds true for the Church. Before we can come into unity, our hearts need to be circumcised. Our sin and veils must be revealed and removed.

The Holy Spirit is within every believer. Each one has a river of living water within. If we can join these rivers together, then we will have a gushing waterfall. Unfortunately, veils hinder the water from flowing out.

They are like sand that traps the anointing within. As a prophet, it is for you to expose and remove that sand so that the anointing can be released freely.

This is why the prophet functions so strongly in the ministry of inner healing. I am not going to get into detail here about how to minister in this way, because I do cover it in the rest of the series, as well as in my book, *The Minister's Handbook*.

As you pray for God's people and minister to them, He will show you the blockages in their lives.

He will show you their roots of bitterness and their fears. When this happens, it is not for the purpose of just tickling their ears. God will not show you these things so that you can "prove" your prophetic call to them.

Rather, He will show you these things because they are veils that stand in the way between that child and the Heavenly Father.

Prophet of God, in moments such as these, you hold in your hand the heart of God's people. Hold it tenderly. There is no more vulnerable moment than when your innermost veils are lifted.

> **KEY PRINCIPLE**
>
> Just as a bride coming into the bridal chamber lifts the veils and feels vulnerable, so also do people feel the same uncertainty when faced with a veil that has to go.

Unfortunately, prophets can be a bit too zealous at times. Instead of handling that heart with care, you can become callous and "dive right in" to tender places that need some care.

So be gentle. Be firm with sin, gentle with hurt, and persistent when you bring healing. With each veil that you help remove from the hearts of God's people, you are preparing them for revival.

Then, when they fellowship with other believers, the anointing within will gush out! For the first time, true unity will be achieved and the corporate anointing will begin to flow.

BRINGING REVIVAL TO THE LOCAL CHURCH

If the Lord has you in a local church right now, and they are open to your ministry, do you realize that you are there to bring revival?

> *KEY PRINCIPLE*
> With each veil you help remove from each person there, you are preparing the way for revival.

You are helping them to open their hearts to one another, allowing the anointing to come out.

The anointing will not just flow from the leadership, but it will also come when God's people cry out as one. Want to bring revival? Start with the hearts around you. Bring unity through healing and removing veils.

3. SHOW THEM THE WAY

Without an example to follow, people will not know how to flow in unity. I am reminded of Miriam who picked up the tambourine and sang a song as the people followed on.

Deborah the prophetess did the same. She sang a song for others to learn and to follow. By doing this, they brought unity!

In the chapters that follow this, I will talk more on your place in bringing unity in praise and worship.

If the Lord has put you up front to lead worship, realize that the focus of this ministry, is to bring unity!

If you have already helped to remove the veils, then lead God's people into the presence of the Lord Jesus. Point the way to Him!

Show them how to pray. Show them how to praise. Show them what Jesus looks like. Be the example you are called to be, and God's people will follow. Revival will be the natural result.

God has something greater for His people, but until you lead them to it, they will never taste it. It is for you to stand up and show them a better way. Start with being the image of Christ, then lead them to take hold of Christ for themselves.

If each prophet had this motivation, we would see a lot more revival in the Church.

When Should Revival Take Place?

We get this idea that revival is for the purpose of bringing in unbelievers. We have been taught for such a long time that revival is for the purpose of spreading the Gospel alone.

However, when I just look at the word "revival," I realize how we have messed this picture up! What does it mean to bring revival? To put it plainly, revival means to bring something back to life, that has died.

In other words, you started a fire and the coals blazed, but now they have gotten cold. Revival means to put more fuel on that fire to cause it to rage once again.

> ***KEY PRINCIPLE***
>
> It is clear why the word "revival" is poorly used if you are trying to use it for the presentation of gospel to unbelievers. Their spirits were never alive to begin with! They do not need to be revived – they need to be born for the first time.

Unbelievers do not need revival – the Church needs revival.

THE PERFECT FIRE STARTER

The cold hearts of God's people need to be ignited once again. The Holy Spirit knows this, and has built the perfect fire starter - the corporate anointing!

He designed it so that when believers get together in unity, the fire falls and ignites their hearts afresh. We should not be seeking God for one-time revivals that soon become a memory of the past.

Rather, this should be something that we receive every time we get together in unity. Your job as a prophet is not to worry about bringing that anointing. Your job is to bring the people into unity, so that the anointing comes down every time that they are gathered!

SIGNS OF DISUNITY

How do you know if there is a blockage in the spirit? It is simple - if you get together in the spirit with any group of believers and the external anointing does not come, then you have some blockages.

They have veils between one another and veils between them and the Lord. If the anointing is lacking, look for veils.

Look for bitterness, fear and guilt. Look for hurts and struggles that cause us to hide our hearts from one another.

The Lord tells us that He is the vine and that we are the branches. We are all connected to one another. When we all connect to Christ, we can expect the fruit to manifest in our lives.

The anointing of the Holy Spirit is a gift to us. The rules to apply are very simple. Sacrifice your veil and experience the power of the Holy Spirit. It is the Lord's built-in mechanism to cause us to enter into the kind of relationship that He desires us to have with one another.

SOME POINTS ON THE ANOINTING

I have covered a lot on the prophetic anointing in this section, along with your responsibility as a prophet. I want to conclude this teaching with some points to remember regarding the anointing as a whole.

ANOINTED ONLY ONCE

Because the Holy Spirit manifests in so many ways, we get the idea that the anointing comes and goes at will. We can often make the mistake of thinking that there are different kinds of anointing that come and go.

When it comes to the internal anointing, you need to realize that the anointing is given only once! The day you got born again, you received the indwelling of the Holy Spirit. You received the anointing!

> *2 Corinthians 1:21 Now He who establishes us with you in Christ and has anointed us is God,*
>
> *22 who also has sealed us and given us the Spirit in our hearts as a guarantee.*

If you dig a bit into the Greek, the word "anointed" in verse 21 is written in the aorist tense. This tense is used when something happens just once – never to be repeated.

> **KEY PRINCIPLE**
>
> In other words, when you were born again and the Holy Spirit was deposited in you – it happened just once!

ANOINTING REMAINS

It is encouraging to know that the anointing remains. We read of Saul, who lost the anointing and his position. I do not think that one of us in ministry, reads that without fear and trembling.

However, you need to realize that this was the Old Testament. Yes, you can certainly lose the external anointing. If there is a veil between you and the Lord, or if you walk in disobedience, you can be sure that you will not experience the external anointing like before.

However, the internal anointing never leaves. Sure, when you are in the flesh, it feels very far from you. When you have veils it seems to be "stuck" but it does not mean it is gone

Consider this passage:

> *1 John 2:27 But the anointing which you have received from Him abides in you, and you do not need that anyone teach you; but as the same*

> *anointing teaches you concerning all things, and is true, and is not a lie, and just as it has taught you, you will abide in Him.*

I love that word "remains." The Holy Spirit does not come one day and leave the next. When He comes to abide inside of you – He remains. He remains to teach you and for as long as you abide in Him, that anointing will be manifested in your life.

Various Manifestations of the Anointing

Now how that anointing manifests in your life will change. Each ministry is different. While the source of the anointing is always the same, the way you operate in it will change.

That is why I have spoken here about the prophetic anointing. Is this an anointing that you will suddenly receive one day? No, you have the Holy Spirit in you already! However, as you start to minister to God's people in this capacity, the anointing inside of you will begin to manifest in a certain way.

As you become the kind of vessel that you need to be, you will also be able to release more anointing than you did before.

With each veil that is removed, and each death to the flesh that you face, your capacity to release what is within will increase.

> **KEY PRINCIPLE**
>
> That is why prophetic training is all about changing who you are! The anointing is within – you just need to be the kind of person that can release it!

THE BRIDGE

So how do the two work together? What exactly happened on the day of Pentecost then? Well, without re-teaching the entire doctrine of the Holy Spirit, let me give you the bottom line.

When the external anointing came on you for the first time, a bridge was formed in the spirit. Whereas before, you just had the indwelling of the Holy Spirit when you got born again. The external anointing caused a bridge to take place where you could enter into a relationship with the Holy Spirit.

It created a pathway between what is within your spirit and outwards through your body – that is why the usual manifestation of this is speaking in tongues! It brought you into a relationship with the Holy Spirit that you did not have before.

Where before, He was the one to renew your spirit, and you came to "abide in Him." Consider 1 John 2:27.

Here John shares how the Holy Spirit will come and abide in you.

Then he ends off by saying, "...you shall abide in him." Well how do you abide in Him if you do not know him? He is in you, but how do you remain in Him? Well that is what is commonly known as the "Baptism of the Holy Spirit!" That is how you came to abide in Him!

As you continued to nurture this relationship with Him and you got around other believers who have this relationship, you can expect Him to show up with an external anointing every time after that!

I like to describe the external anointing as "topping up" your spirit when it feels dry! As you go through life, your experience and knowledge of the Lord starts to develop a gap!

You know the Lord is there, but you do not experience Him a lot of the time in your day-to-day walk. Your inner stream feels empty and you feel weary. When you experience the external anointing, it brings you back to life.

CONVICTION OF SIN

It removes all the veils that have crept into your life! Suddenly the anointing within gushes out and you feel filled all over again! What just happened there? Did you ever notice how the first thing to take place with the external anointing is the conviction of sin?

The external anointing burns away those veils, allowing your spirit to feel topped up again!

Come to Rest

In a church age where so many are "searching" for the anointing, it is my desire to bring you to rest. You already have it! Every believer does!

All you need to do, is to go through the process to let more out. God is not about to "take away" the anointing within simply because you did not perform for Him. He is not an earthly father that would spite you.

Above all, if you feel thirsty, and are lacking the reality of the anointing in your life – then you need a top up!

You have allowed the things of this world to weigh you down. You have allowed cares, fears, and bitter thoughts to put veils up that are preventing you from feeling the Lord.

Strip the veils. Then get together with another believer and get into unity. Get revived again. It is God's gift to you and He will not withhold it. Then when you are on fire and ready to "take on the hordes of hell" again – step out and revive the Church!

PART 02

PROPHETIC PRAYER AND INTERCESSION

Part 02 – Prophetic Prayer and Intercession

Introduction to Prophetic Intercession

If you have been around the prophetic block a bit, you are probably thinking, "You know what, I know everything that there is to know about prophetic intercession." There are so many books on it, but I guarantee that by the end of this part - you are going to be challenged to see intercession in a way you haven't before.

I think that the military structure of most countries look the same. There is a certain hierarchy to the way things run.

For example, at the bottom of the pecking order, you have the private who is still wet behind the ears. At the top, you have the general with a few medals weighing down his shoulders.

Now in this hierarchy there is an order to things. The private does not leave his ranks and tell his fellow soldiers what to do. Could you imagine being in the middle of warfare when one of the privates pushes his way to the front to give orders?

How many men do you think would follow him? It would not matter how good his ideas were. Unless he was given the license to give those orders from his superior - that private's words mean nothing.

Now let that same private have a signed document from his general and things would change completely. If he had the authority of his general to speak, then the platoon had better listen.

Things change because the men are not obeying the private any longer – they are taking orders from the general. The private is just the messenger.

What has this got to do with intercession? More than you realize! As a prophet, without the authority from your higher authority, your words mean nothing. No demon, no person, no angel, no circumstance... nobody is going to listen to you.

Without authority, you can pray 24 hours a day and not have any results.

Jesus is Your General

The purpose of intercession is to release God's will into the earth. So it stands to reason, that unless you are speaking God's words, nothing is going to happen. You need to know what God wants, and you need to get to the place where you can hear Him so clearly that when you speak, that they aren't your words.

There are some misconceptions of what intercession is. One of them being to bombard the heavens until God just relents and gives you what you want.

Nothing could be further from the truth. The objective of prophetic intercession is to get into the Throne Room, and to pray down from heaven.

If you want to see results to your prayer, instead of trying to "reach God" from "down here," you need to be seated in heavenly places and pray from heaven!

When you get to the Throne Room, you stand in His authority. That's when the fun begins. That is where you start the process of intercession.

THE 5 FUNCTIONS OF PRAYER AND INTERCESSION

I love that ours is a God of such variety! There are many ways to come to the Lord in prayer, but for this section, we are going to look at 5 specific ways.

As you master each one, you will see how they build on one another. If you have not seen results to your prayers and intercession, then you are about to go through a spiritual revolution!

As we look at each function, I will be helping you separate the difference between prayer, and intercession. I understand how confusing this can be. It is this very confusion that has drained the power from prayer in the Church!

When you pray, instead of interceding, you will fail to be led correctly. When you intercede instead of praying, you will miss out on moments of intimacy with Jesus.

Prophetic Prayer and Intercession

As a prophet you need to master both prayer and intercession! With that being said, let's look at the 5 functions of prayer and intercession.

THESE 5 FUNCTIONS ARE AS FOLLOWS:

1. Prayer of Praise
2. Prayer of Petition
3. Persistent Prayer
4. Intercessory Warfare
5. Intercessory Decree

Master all five of these and you will shake the foundations of the earth! You have learned to hear the voice of God, and by now you should be flowing well in revelation. Now all you need to learn, is how to take that revelation and use it to get results in intercession.

In the next chapter, I will introduce the subject of prayer to give you the key principles you need to start becoming effective right now in your prayer life.

From there, I will take you on a journey to mastering all 5 prayer functions. Start expecting miracles in your life. What you have prayed for, for years, is about to come to pass!

Chapter 05

Prophetic Prayer 101

Chapter 05 – Prophetic Prayer 101

> *Amos 3:7 Surely the Lord God does nothing, unless He reveals His secret to His servants the prophets.*

Anyone can pray. In fact, any believer should and can pray with effective results. So what makes you different? Well, what sets you apart are some of the tools that you use for the purpose of prayer and intercession.

What makes you different? The anointing and authority is what sets you apart. So then the question remains, how do we get to the anointing?

Well to get the anointing flowing, you need to go to the source. You have to go into the Throne Room. When you are in the Throne Room, and the anointing is in your words, you can speak two words of power and they will go forth as a double-edged sword that divides and does not return void.

It is a lot easier than standing "down here," and shouting words for hours without any anointing at all.

Why do it the hard way? Let's not be stupid here. Think back to all the times that you have prayed, interceded, and sought God on behalf of others. Thinking back now, ask yourself, "How many of these prayer times were really anointed?"

How many times did you just rush through your list? Perhaps you can identify with the camp that rushes through everything to try and just get it all "out there." That camp that thinks that if you pray and pray, that eventually the fervent prayer of the saints would avail much.

> **KEY PRINCIPLE**
>
> Yes, the fervent prayers of the just will avail much, but the anointed prayer of the prophet avails even more.

You stand as a watchman on the wall. You should speak the right word in season, with the anointing. When you do that, you are going to see change.

It took just one great shout to bring down the walls of Jericho. Why? It was the power that brought those walls down.

What is going to bring the change to your prayer life? What is going to bring change to the church? You, flapping your lips for hours every day in prayer?

Keep praying like that and perhaps you will see an answer to your prayer in the next twenty years! No, those words are empty, unless they contain that "extra something." Without the anointing, your words are just strings of letters thrown around at random unless they contain the fire of God. This kind of fire is only found in the Throne Room of God.

WRONG IDEA: THE MORE THE MERRIER

There is also a failure I see that says, "If I have a need, the more people I get to pray for me the better." I can't tell you how many prayer requests we get a day. Not that I mind, but you know that these are folks that browsed the internet and found every single ministry site that they could to post their little prayer request to.

Their logic is this, "If I can get a lot of people praying, then it will twist God's arm and He has to answer my prayer.

Obviously, God listens to some people more than to others. So we just need to keep asking often. Then, as God is sitting 'up there' in His Throne Room and He hears a choir of prayers coming up, He might incline His ear to that prayer and answer me."

Logically, we know that this is not the case, but still, this is the thinking that is out there. Somebody has a need, so they ask every church in the area to pray. They ask every intercessor and every minister they know.

ONE WORD AT THE RIGHT TIME IS POWERFUL

I am not saying it is wrong to stand in agreement, because when you know your authority, this kind of agreement has the power to bring change.

However, if you have 200 people praying empty words - nothing will happen.

> **KEY PRINCIPLE**
>
> The secret to effective prayer is not in quantity, but in authority!

On the other hand, you could have one prophet standing in the anointing, praying the right word at the right time, and you will see miracles.

Do you want to see change? Stop trying to gather hundreds of people to pray. You just need two or three. The scripture says,

> *Matthew 18:20 For where two or three are gathered together in My name, I am there in the midst of them.*

If you want the maximum power to see something happen, then two or three need to speak with the anointing.

ENTER THE THRONE ROOM

The Lord showed it to me like this once. As I was praying in the spirit, I saw how the words were coming out of my mouth. As they left my lips, I saw how His anointing came on them like fire on the outside. Suddenly those words became arrows and went into the hearts of God's people.

I realized that, in myself, they were just words. They were just my thoughts and my feelings. Let's be honest, as prophets, we often mix all our own stuff in there.

We all make mistakes, but when God can take our words and anoint them, then they will always hit the mark. They will go into the earth and they will not return void. That's the whole purpose of prophetic prayer.

When you enter the Throne Room, not only are you going to speak with anointing, but you are going to see as God sees. You can come to the Lord with a concern or a thought on your mind and you think, "I don't know how God is going to perform this miracle."

You come with a conflict in your heart and you think, "Lord, I don't think that I am ever going to win this battle. I don't think that I am ever going to overcome this problem."

But when you just quiet down, get into His presence, and see things from His eyes, looking down from the

Throne Room, your problem looks like a little heap of sand. What looked like a big mountain from your personal perspective, from the Throne Room, is nothing but a molehill.

That is why you have to get into His presence first. Think of the last meeting that you attended where you sensed the presence of the Lord, or when you experienced the anointing. It felt so good. In that moment, everything was possible.

No matter how big the mountain is, when you experience the anointing, your thinking changes.

You start to think, "I can do this even though I had a tough week. Everything is possible!" You begin to see things through God's eyes, and the impossible becomes possible.

You keep making the mistake by asking, "Lord, what's your will? Lord, what should I do? Lord, what is going on?"

If you just entered into His Throne Room, more often you would know what was going on.

You would see as God sees. You would understand and then you would be able to speak what He shows you. You would clearly know the direction that He has given.

SET ASIDE THE WEIGHTS

So, here you are. You come to the Lord in prayer and intercession, and you have got your list in hand. Your fears, cares, and concerns are like bulging suitcases scattered all around you.

In them are housed all the problems that came up this week, along with the financial and health needs that you have.

On top of all that, you also have everybody else out there that has needs and problems. You have circumstances that are coming at you right now, and you don't know whether to turn left or right. The truth is, you don't even know how to start praying.

The first thing, you need to do, is let all that baggage go.

When I come to intercede, my prayer is something along the following lines:

"Lord, I submit myself to you, I let go of my cares, burdens, what I think, and all my problems."

"I just put everything at your feet and I let it all go."

"I make myself a vessel for you Lord. Let me speak your words. Let me speak with your power. "

When you get to the place of being able to enter into His Throne Room, it gets easier every time you pray. Every time after that, you don't have to try hard as hard. It becomes much easier to get into His presence, because you know how to get into unity with the Lord.

The first time you try this, it will take a little while. Often you have so many thoughts rolling around in your head that it takes a while to get rid of all the junk that keeps coming to your mind.

Take all the time you need to dump all that baggage, because it is very important before you even begin praying, that you throw away all your needs and worries. You can't afford any bitterness, you can't afford any guilt, and you can't afford any fear.

You need to apply

> *Hebrews 12:1 Therefore we also, since we are surrounded by so great a cloud of witnesses, let us lay aside every weight, and the sin which so easily ensnares us, and let us run with endurance the race that is set before us,*

By throwing aside all the weights that are dragging you down, you will find it easy to get into His presence to pray.

So let it all go. You will be surprised, by the end of interceding, to find that those things are sorted out without you even having to pray for them.

Just by being in the Throne Room, and seeing as God sees, you understand things like He understands them.

Only Pray What God Shows You

Perhaps this is a bit self-explanatory, but I will say it anyway. Pray only what God tells you to pray. The idea of going into the Throne Room is to see as God sees. When you see what God sees, you only pray what He says.

You will learn later on, that you can bring a list to the Lord in prayer, but even then, you should only pray through what He tells you to.

Prophetic Intercession is even more cut and dry. If the Lord has called you to intercession, then the list stays at home. Dump every idea you have, and come to see what God has in mind for you to speak forth.

You know, the awesome thing is, when you only pray what God shows, it is going to be anointed and will hit the mark every time.

When you come to pray with this mindset, you will be surprised to find yourself praying things that you didn't think that you were going to pray.

Get Revelation!

Good! You shouldn't leave a time of intercession thinking, "That's what I thought God would say." If that is the case, then you didn't get revelation. Sorry, it doesn't work that way. Get your own thinking out of the way.

When you pray what God shows you, you will always pray in the right time, you will always hit the mark, and you will always have results.

> **KEY PRINCIPLE**
> 1. Pray with anointing
> 2. Pray only what God shows you

Those two principles are like a cold front and a warm front combining into a hurricane. When that happens, it will create a storm in the heavens that is going to react and bring change to your life and to this earth.

Imagine if all intercessors prayed with this power. Imagine if every intercessor prayed from the Throne Room!

If we prayed with power, anointing, and what God wanted us to pray, we would see a change in the body of Christ as we have never seen it.

PRAYER VS. INTERCESSION

> *1 Timothy 2:1 Therefore I exhort first of all that supplications, prayers, intercessions, and giving of thanks be made for all men;*

I want to help bring a dividing line between what you see with many "prayer lines," and what God has called you to do as a prophet.

Prayer is something every believer should engage in, so if intercession and prayer are the same thing, then what defines you as a prophet?

Well that is exactly what the passage in 1 Timothy 2:1 helps us sort out. It helps us to begin to understand the difference between prayer and intercession. Let's dig into *Strong's* for a bit and look up what the word "prayer" means here.

> 4335
>
> proseuche {pros-yoo-khay'}
>
> AV - prayer 36, pray earnestly + 3346 1; 37
>
> 1) prayer addressed to God

Note that the first difference is that prayer is always directed to the Lord. Your words leave your heart and reach the ears of the Lord. They are sent upward. When you grasp this simple concept, intercession begins to take on a much bigger meaning to you.

> 1783
>
> enteuxis {ent'-yook-sis}
>
> AV - intercession 1, prayer 1; 2
>
> 1) a falling in with, meeting with
>
> 1a) converse or for any other cause

1b) a conference or conversation

> **KEY PRINCIPLE**
>
> Simply put, prayer is addressed to God, while intercession is God's will conveyed and released on behalf of others.

Everyone knows how to pray! They send their prayers up to heaven like incense. That prayer moves the heart of the Lord. Did you ever wonder how the answers are going to come back down though? Well that is where we need to start decreeing the will of God into the earth!

Prayers are not answered when they go up. They are simply heard. Prayers are answered when they are sent back down! This is what I am going to teach you in the next few chapters. I will teach you how to put that answer from the Lord into your mouth and to send it back down to the earth!

INTERCESSION DEFINITION

Intercession involves a "back and forth" between you and the Lord. In other words, it is the time when God gets to say what He wants to do in your life. Intercession is words that are sent downward.

If you want to intercede with power, you need to move past "just praying." In other words, you need to move past just bringing your words to the Lord and get to the place where He is giving you His words to release into this earth.

Instead of always praying upward towards heaven, you must learn to intercede downwards from the heavenly realm!

> **KEY PRINCIPLE**
>
> That is why the first principle for intercession is this: You do not come to the Lord with a prayer list. You come to the Lord to get a prayer list.

The other defining characteristic of intercession is, that you do not pray on your behalf! If you look at our definition again, you will see how it refers to having a conversation or of pleading someone else's case.

As an intercessor you are like a lawyer, presenting someone's case to the judge. Is this not what Jesus does for us at the right hand of the Father all the time? He pleads our case for us. He does not plead his own case!

This is also where intercession changes from prayer. In prayer, you are bringing your own needs before the

Lord. In intercession, you are holding up God's people before Him. Not only are you coming to make a request on their behalf, but you are also allowing the Lord to use you to plead on their behalf according to His will!

In the next chapter I am going to show you why the Lord needs you to be His mouthpiece and why you are called to not only be in the battlefront on behalf of others, but also to be the watchman on the wall.

CHAPTER 06

WORDS OF POWER

Chapter 06 – Words of Power

"Sticks and stones may break my bones, but words will never harm me." I can still hear this chorus echoing in my mind as we sang it as twelve-year-olds in retaliation to the playground bully.

No words could be further from the truth though. Words carry a power that can hurt or heal us more than anything else. When you think back on memories of the past, it is the words of encouragement that make you smile. It is the words of shame you remember that make you cringe.

In fact, whether we want to admit it or not, words carry a power that affects us very deeply. This is even truer when it comes to the realm of the Spirit. There is a reason why words carry so much punch. The explanation of it is very simple.

Why Words Count

Consider how I taught in *The Prophetic Functions* book, how man is made up of spirit, soul and body. Now we all know that the Holy Spirit comes to dwell in the spirit of man. We are His temple!

So right within you is all the anointing you will ever need to bring real change to this world. You contain an atom bomb inside of you that is set to revolutionize the world! With clear direction, revelation, and a right word in season, you have the makings of a spiritual bomb inside of you!

There is no doubt that the anointing brings change on this earth. There is no doubt that the Holy Spirit has the power to move mountains. However, how will you release that power?

The most powerful bomb in this natural world is useless unless it is activated. So tell me, where is your "activation" switch for your spiritual bomb?

The answer lies in this powerful scripture.

> *Mark 11:23 'I tell you the truth, if anyone says to this mountain, 'Go, throw yourself into the sea,' and does not doubt in his heart but believes that what he says will happen, it will be done for him.*
>
> *24 Therefore I tell you, whatever you ask for in prayer, believe that you have received it, and it will be yours. (NIV)*

We all know that faith moves mountains. Faith is undoubtedly an atom bomb! What releases that faith though? Well the little switch that turns all of that faith into a bomb lies in the words, "If anyone says..."

Words are the secret switch to release what is inside of you. In fact, it is both words and actions that take what is inside of you and releases it at the mountains in your life.

Your Activation Switch

When you begin to grasp this concept, you will have some soul searching to do. Sometimes you keep silent and do not speak out the things you believe. On the other hand, you often find yourself saying things that only make your mountains bigger. Regardless of how you use your words, I want you to know this:

> **Key Principle**
>
> Your words hold the activation switch of power. Flick that switch wisely!

What I also love about this passage is how beautifully it conveys the principle I shared at the end of the previous chapter. This kind of prayer is doing a lot more than just praying, "Lord please remove the mountains out of my life."

Rather this kind of prayer is saying, "You! Mountain! Be removed!"

This changes everything. It means that you can, by a choice of your own, release a spiritual force against the mountains in your life and in the lives of others.

Did you know that there are many in this world who know about this secret power that the Lord has put into man? The world calls it the "power of positive thinking" and just by remaining positive and saying that things will be good, they will turn out good.

Did you ever wonder how that is even possible for unbelievers to change their lives? It is because human beings have a spirit inside of them. The Lord made us in His image remember? We have a human spirit and this spirit has dominion over this world.

Now if someone, by using their sheer will power alone, can bring about changes to their life, how much more a blood-bought child of Christ?

Then to push this forward even further – how much more change can you bring, as a prophet, with a powerful anointing from God?

Your potential to bring change in the Church and this world is limitless! But do you know what the problem is? You keep forgetting to speak to the mountain. You keep crying out to God about your mountain instead of believing that God wants the mountain removed and then telling it to leave!

INTERCESSION: SAYING IT RIGHT

This is one of the key points that I want you to learn regarding true intercession. I want you to learn to find your words!

Now this might sound strange at first, but stick with me here. So often, you make the mistake of sending hundreds of words "up to heaven" instead of saying powerful words that are directed towards what God wants you to pray about.

In the chapter on decree, I am going to teach you a bit more about how to "speak to the mountains," but for now let me give you some practical things to start applying to your life.

FATHER GOD, JESUS GOD, SPIRIT, JESUS, LORD

Just because your words contain power, it does not mean the more you say, the more power you have. In fact, there is an easy way to hemorrhage any power and authority that you might have in prayer. The way to drain any anointing fast is to babble off using meaningless words.

The first thing that I teach any one of our trainers when they become a part of our team, is to pay attention to the words they use when they pray. More often than not, they do not know how to approach the Lord and so try to fit as many of His names as possible into their prayer.

So they might sound a little like this:

"Thank you Jesus Father God, for being with us God. Spirit, Jesus there is a mountain before me God. Sweet Father, Jesus please can you take this mountain God. Remove this mountain Jesus. Father, Jesus, Son of God, please answer us today God!"

What a headache! Know anyone that prays this way? Would you be gutsy enough to record one of your own prayers and count now many times you throw out "useless words" because you simply do not know what to say?

I am going to tell you something that I sure hope you never forget.

Here it is: The Lord knows His own name.

When you pray, the Lord hears your heart. In fact, the Scriptures say that even before you pray, He has already heard you! So in truth, you really do not need to labor the point of calling out to every one of His names in the hope that He will answer you quicker!

In fact, all your words will do is distract you from what you really need to hear. For the rest of us next to you, we are having a really hard time following what you are saying. In the end, all everyone hears is your emotion, and knows without a doubt that you know that Jesus is God.

BRINGING IT BACK TO BASICS

To change your prayer to make it effective right now, just bring it back to basics. Talk to Jesus like He is sitting right next to you. He is in you. He is around you. He permeates everything you see and touch in this world!

Take a breath and reach out to Him in faith instead of abundant words. You will find your spirit start to come to rest and you will hear and see things in the spirit that you so often miss.

When you are caught up in "praying hard," you will drown out the words and impressions of the Holy Spirit trying to bubble up from deep within you.

Yes, our words contain power. However, how much power would you like today? In ages past, they used bows and arrows for warfare. Today we use bombs and guns. Which is more devastating? Would you like a bow and arrow in your prayer, or would you like to blast that mountain out of the way with a well-placed bomb?

It is up to you, really. Sure, you could "Thank you Jesus God, Father, God…" for an hour. Using this method, you would send hundreds of arrows against that mountain and eventually, over much time, it might start to move.

Or, you could say, "Mountain! Be removed" with faith and authority, and you could level that thing in one prayer! It is up to you, really.

> **KEY PRINCIPLE**
>
> Your words as a prophet and intercessor carry power. How much power, really depends on you.

Firstly, you need the anointing, which you will get in the Throne Room of God. Secondly, you need faith, which you get from hearing His rhema word. What you need most of all though, is to speak forth the words that will release both forces at the problem.

So what kind of words do you release when you pray? Let me see if I can help you find those words to start praying effectively right now!

FINDING YOUR WORDS

I already shared with you that prayer is making your request known to the Lord. Intercession is a "back and forth" to get God's answer down.

That is why the first part of the intercessory process is coming before the Lord with your care, need, or by His leading. Before you can start telling the mountains to be removed, you need to find out if this mountain belongs there or not! Once you know His will, the anointing is easy enough.

So that is why you need to pray. Your first step in prayer should sound like this,

"Lord Jesus I see this mountain in our lives. What do you want us to do with it?"

Now is the time to apply everything that you learned in the *Prophetic Functions* book. As you bring your request to the Lord, does He say "yes" or "no?" Did you receive a vision or a word of knowledge? Whatever it was, you will get an answer from Him.

Once you get the answer from the Lord, it is time to stop praying to the Lord, and time to start speaking to that mountain! If the Lord shows you that the mountain has to go, you need to look at that mountain from the heavenly realm and say,

"In the name of Jesus! Mountain be removed!"

Now the worst thing that you can do at this point is to keep praying to God to remove the mountain! What does our scripture say in Mark 11:23? It says, "Whoever says to this mountain…" It does not say, "…if God says to this mountain."

If you prayed, and God gave you the go-ahead to remove the mountain, then He just allocated some of His authority to you! He gave you license to tell that mountain to leave. It is for you to speak to that mountain now – not the Lord.

> **KEY PRINCIPLE**
>
> This is the second most power-draining mistake made during intercession: to keep asking God to move the mountain, when He told you to do it!

You pray. God says, "Take that mountain down."

You continue to pray, "Thank you Lord for removing this mountain."

Well no wonder it did not move! Not even a little shake. Stop telling the Lord what He already knows, and talk to the mountain!

"Mountain be removed!"

"I call these circumstances into line according to the will of God!"

"I bind every work of the enemy!"

"I call forth the finances right now! Healing you be manifest right now!"

Prayer With Purpose

Now that is what I call "flipping the switch!" Prayer like that has purpose!

Not only are you standing in the authority and revelation that God has given to you, but you are putting your spiritual atom bomb to work.

This simple change in the way you pray will turn your prayer life upside down. Try it, and see what kind of results you get.

Not only that, but you will receive more revelation, and be used of the Lord more often than before.

So to bring it all together:

1. Make Your Words Count

Cut out unnecessary "filler" words in your prayers. Stop repeating the Lord's name over and over again. His blood is enough to justify you – you do not need to prove yourself.

2. Give Your Words Purpose

Once the Lord has given you a direction to pray, direct your prayers to the problem at hand. Do not keep praying for something God already gave you the authority to uproot or to plant.

Stop sending your prayers "upward" and start speaking "downward," giving your prayers focus.

These simple two principles are like charging and activating a spiritual bomb. All that is left to do, is for you to get out there and to blast some mountains out of the way!

CHAPTER 07

THE 1ST FUNCTION OF PRAYER: PRAISE

Chapter 07 – The 1st Function of Prayer: Praise

It is no secret that praise is a source of power! Especially for us prophets! You could have had the worst day ever, but in just a few minutes of praise and worship, you are ready to take on the hordes of hell again!

It is no surprise then that praise is one of the most powerful weapons to be used in the process of prayer and intercession. Not only does it take you into the Throne Room of God, but it contains the anointing to release the will of God into the earth.

Praise in the Word – Jehoshaphat and David

Jehoshaphat sure knew about it. When the Lord said that He would win a war on the behalf of the people, the musicians were sent ahead to praise. Take a look at what happened:

> *2 Chronicles 20:21 And when he had consulted with the people, he appointed those who should sing to the Lord, and who should praise the beauty of holiness, as they went out before the army and were saying: "Praise the Lord, for His mercy endures forever."*
>
> *22 Now when they began to sing and to praise, the Lord set ambushes against the people of*

> *Ammon, Moab, and Mount Seir, who had come against Judah; and they were defeated.*

David was also well aware of the power praise had in prayer. You read of how much time he spent on his harp while looking after the sheep. It is no surprise then that when he stood to face Goliath, that he did so full of the power of God. Praise builds up your faith. It infuses you with the anointing.

PROPHETIC PRAISE

Praise works, because it takes the power of the enemy away. When you praise the Lord, regardless of what is going on in your life, you take away the sting that the enemy is inflicting on you right now. You can turn even the most difficult situation into a reason to praise the Lord – thus putting Him in control of your problem!

It helps you to see things from God's perspective. Praise also gets your spirit, soul and body focused on the same thing!

You are singing with your body, including your mind, emotions, and will into the act, which opens a door for your spirit to flow out freely.

No wonder you love praise and worship so much! There might be times when the Lord will have you just worship in the spirit for the entire time of intercession.

You can sing in tongues and let your spirit do all the intercession. Take the time to master this way of entering into the Throne Room.

Not only does praise allow you to get into the Throne Room faster, but it is also a fantastic weapon of warfare.

In fact, when I do spiritual warfare, I do it best with my guitar in hand!

> **KEY PRINCIPLE**
>
> Praise aligns your spirit, soul, and body. It focuses your eyes on Jesus and does not leave any room for doubt.

The melody fills your heart, and the words of praise fill your mind. There is no place for the enemy to sneak in. Praise is often illustrated as the burning of incense in Scripture.

The Word also says that the Lord inhabits the praises of His people! So when you praise, you are sending incense up to the Lord. In return, He releases His anointing right back.

You start experiencing a back and forth between your spirit and the very Throne Room of God! Do not neglect the use of praise before entering into intercession.

If you are simply committing the day to the Lord, or seeking the Lord concerning a crisis situation, begin with praise. Get your mind, emotions, and will in line with the Lord Jesus and pray from there. See His face, hear His voice, and feel His heartbeat. Praise allows you to do that.

Before you know it, you will find yourself in His Throne Room. It is only once you are there that you can begin to pray.

How to get Into His Throne Room

It is the desire of every prophet to see results when you pray. You already know that to get that power, you need to find your way to the Throne Room of God.

Sometimes you might feel like a mouse running around in a maze that has been booby-trapped! Perhaps you keep finding yourself getting lost when you take a left and "zapped" when you take a right. There is an easy way though to enter into His Throne Room. As you work on this chapter and the ones that follow, you will find the map you have been looking for.

Let us bypass the traps, save you the hassle of "getting lost along the way," and lead you right into the presence of the Father!

So now that I have convinced you that you need to get into the Throne Room…how do you go about it?

1. Put Aside Your Burdens

The point is that you want to get yourself to a place where you can let go of all your burdens and cares.

Some people like to go for a walk on the beach. Others like to find a quiet spot in the garden. It is really up to you. How do you get into the presence of the Lord? Because intercession is an "other orientation", you need to put down what is burdening you right now.

That might mean just praising and putting every care on the cross. It might mean going for a walk to step away from circumstances that are putting pressure on you. The point is, that your focus needs to change from your cares and on to what God wants to do.

2. Quiet Your Spirit

This follows on from the last point. Once you have put your cares aside, pray in a quiet place. If the kids are shouting and the phone ringing, you will be distracted. Find a place where you can have peace – even if that place is in the bathroom! Hey, do not knock it – I have had some anointed moments in the Throne Room right from my bathtub!

3. Change the Pictures

While your mind is distracted by your cares, you will not be able to see what God wants you to pray. When I

The 1st Function of Prayer: Praise

enter into intercession, I find it really helpful to bring to mind past visions the Lord gave me in His presence.

I might see myself walking with Jesus next to a stream or I might see myself standing in the Throne Room. If you need a little help with some pictures to help you focus on what you are doing, I recommend you get hold of *The Journey of Tamar*. There I paint the pictures the Lord has given me of the Throne Room over the years.

4. Talk to the Lord Jesus

It is a bad habit to start times of intercession by jumping into warfare and just shouting at the devil. Rather take time to see the Lord Jesus in front of you and talk to Him. Welcome Him and ask Him to show you what He wants.

> **Key Principle**
>
> Do not just "talk in the spirit" but talk to a person! Jesus is real and when you treat Him accordingly – feeling His presence is the natural outcome.

I know that sometimes, as prophets, we can get all too excited about kicking the devil's butt. In the next chapters I will certainly cover that point, but before you head out for war, it is a good idea to drop a line to your general first. It is easy to get distracted with the spiritual warfare all around you, that you forget that the solution to it all is not your prayer, but the power of Christ.

If you start by simply "opening up" conversation between you and the Lord, you will be amazed at how easy it is to get a healthy "back and forth" going. However, if you leap directly into decree or warfare, you will be in danger of missing a gentle nudging in a different direction.

It does not take very long to say, "Lord Jesus I thank you for calling me into this special time. You are so precious to me and I look forward to the things you are about to show me."

5. Get Into the Anointing

Like I already said before, what always helps me enter into the Throne Room, is to start with praise and worship. I find that probably for myself, that's the best way. Every one of us is different. Perhaps you like praying in tongues, there are some that just like to commit themselves to the Lord. I like to pick up my guitar.

In later chapters, I will teach you more about how to use music in prayer and spiritual warfare, but for now it is important that you know how powerful this tool is.

When you worship the Lord, you cannot help but put aside your burdens. Music carries you to another place and cuts out the rest of the noise. It allows you to find the peace in the storm.

When you sing songs it also changes the pictures rummaging around in your head. Instead of being distracted with bad thoughts, you will see the pictures that you are singing about instead.

This also helps you to converse with Jesus. If you sing songs of worship, you are engaged in a conversation with the Lord.

Not only is it a powerful weapon of warfare, but in a few songs, I can be ushered into the Throne Room. When you praise the Lord, you are offering up incense and in return, you will feel the presence of the Lord come on you.

START PRAYING WHEN...

Do not start praying until you sense the anointing. Do not pray until you get the pictures from the Lord. They may come in various forms and we have already covered this in *The Prophetic Functions* book. You may get visions, words of knowledge, or words of wisdom. Do not pray until you have His anointing on you.

I remember when the Lord first gave us this revelation. I tell you, it revolutionized my prayer life. I was so excited about praying. I wanted to pray all the time just to see if it would work again. I knew how to get into the anointing. Especially as a prophet, you pick up the guitar and the Holy Spirit is there.

So I knew how to get into His presence, but the thought of using this anointing for prayer is what blew my mind. It is exciting and the best part is that it really works. Try it.

Pray For the Fun of It

Throw away the list and allow the anointing to inspire you! That's my challenge for you right now. Don't intercede as a chore, do it for the pure joy of being used as a vessel to speak what God wants into this earth.

He could be using you to transform things all around you.

> **Key Principle**
>
> That is what intercession is about: to bring miracles to pass. To take the Word of God, and to create something out of nothing.

That is the most exciting part of all. Not only will your times in the presence of the Lord make you spiritually fit, but they will bring real results. What an incredible investment. You could be fulfilling your purpose as a prophet right now – so run into His presence and turn this world upside down.

CHAPTER 08

THE 2ND FUNCTION: PETITION

Chapter 08 – The 2ⁿᵈ Function: Petition

> *Philippians 4:6 Be anxious for nothing, but in everything by prayer and supplication, with thanksgiving, let your requests be made known to God.*

Everybody has a contact. You know, that one person that could do a favor for you if you needed them to.

My husband is probably one of the best contacts that you could have, because he knows everybody and everybody knows him. He also knows a little bit about everything. So if ever you need something done or have a question - he is usually a pretty good contact to have. You could go to him and say, "Hey Craig, could you organize this for me?" or "Do you know where I could find… ?"

He probably knows somewhere or someone where you could organize what you need.

Well, as prophets we have the ultimate contact of all. His name is the Lord Jesus Christ. With Him, the best thing is that He really does have everything, and He really does know everyone.

Mastering Petitionary Prayer

There is a thing about asking somebody a favor though. If I come to Craig and I say, "Hey love, there is this friend of mine and she would like some help with transferring her data to a new computer... " It is up to Craig to grant me the favor for my friend. That seems logical, doesn't it?

That is a good picture of what petitionary prayer is all about. This kind of prayer is going to your "contact" on behalf of others. In essence, you are going to the Lord Jesus and saying, "Lord, would you mind doing me a favor? I have a friend who is really sick right now. Would you mind helping out?"

Then it is for God to grant the request or not. You would be amazed to find out how many people don't see it this way at all. They think that because they bring a prayer list to God that God is obligated to answer it.

God does want to answer and certainly if your request lines up with His Word, of course He wants to answer. He desires to. However, the timing and how He answers is really up to Him. People seem to forget that. They think that if they nag God again and again that He will give them what they want.

> **KEY PRINCIPLE**
>
> > The definition of petitionary prayer is: Bringing your request to the Lord and waiting for His answer.

I have already taught you to burn your prayer list when coming to the Lord in intercession. However, there are times when there are things on your mind – a care when somebody is sick or needs a miracle.

At times like this, you can go to your contact, the Lord Jesus, and say, "Hey Lord, would you mind helping me out with this?"

It is perfectly acceptable. What happens after that though is where you need to change the way you think. It doesn't mean that just because you brought it to the Lord that He has to answer right away.

You can bring your petitionary prayer to Him, but then you need to be sensitive enough in the spirit to sense whether He is saying, "Yes, pray for it" or "No."

RULES OF ENGAGEMENT

The first step in bringing any of this to the Lord though is to enter into the Throne Room. Use praise and worship to get into His presence. Put your list aside for now, and allow Him to speak.

You know, it is polite, that when you are in the company of a person that is a higher authority than you, that you let them speak first.

1. LET GOD SPEAK FIRST

So let's be nice to the Lord and allow Him the place of glory and honor that He deserves. Let Him speak first. This is always good protocol to follow in intercession.

When you do this, you will find your prayer following a natural order.

Go to the Lord. He will give you some words to speak, and then speak them. When He is finished speaking, you are more than welcome to come to the Lord with your petitionary prayer and say, "Lord, my sister is not well. Father, I need your help with my marriage. Father, we have a financial need." Whatever the care is, whatever comes to your mind, bring it up to the Lord.

2. Listen to His "Yes" or "No"

One of two things is going to happen. Either you are going to feel a Thummim or a Urim. The Urim is a "yes, yes, okay, pray for this" and the Thummim feels like a knot in your stomach. Your words fall to the ground the moment they leave your mouth.

You say, "Lord, I'd like to bring my... ugh" and you can barely finish the sentence because there is no flow at all. Drop it. God does not want you to pray about this right now.

I think that sometimes we put ourselves under too much pressure as prophets. We think that because we are spokesmen for the Lord, and we speak prophetically that we have to get revelation all the time.

You put yourself under the pressure of always having to speak the Word and bring a miracle to pass as if God is just there as a necessary extra.

> **KEY PRINCIPLE**
>
> If God does not want you to pray, then He has a purpose for it. Maybe that person's faith is lacking, or maybe you are not praying in the right direction.

The point is, God is in charge here. Don't try and push through just because you have a need or care. If God says, "Drop it!" then drop it!

I tell you what is fantastic. When you bring something to the Lord and you feel a "yeah, this is the time to pray for it." When you open your mouth, revelation and the anointing flows.

You will feel a surge in the spirit, followed by a flow in all the gifts of the Spirit. It will feel like a dam has burst.

When you bring a request to the Lord and this happens, then know that you are on the right track. Follow it through until it stops. Then bring your next petition to Him.

3. Pray in Line With His Will

This is really fun when you are praying in a group, because you can back one another up. Perhaps you have experienced this yourself already.

Imagine this case scenario. You are praying in a group and the Lord's presence is there. The anointing is present and the revelation is flowing out naturally from you all. Then someone in the group brings something else before the Lord and it feels as if the waters suddenly dry up.

From a gushing waterfall, you feel a spiritual drought. The revelation stops flowing. Death. Silence.

The worst thing you can do when this happens is to push through with that word. Stop right there. The Lord is saying, "no." He is saying, "Get in line with my plan." You need to get in line with God's agenda here. He has a very clear plan for every one of us.

It is not for you to tell God what He needs to answer and when. You need to learn to let God be in control and learn to pray in faith. Let me tell you, there is nothing more exciting than when you bring a care to the Lord, and you feel the anointing.

It is exhilarating when you feel that surge and your faith explodes. When this happens, there is no doubt that when you speak, things are going to happen!

> **KEY PRINCIPLE**
>
> If you try to push through in the flesh, you are going to leave your prayer time very tired and very discouraged. The only way to pray in faith, is to make sure that you are praying according to His will.

You have got a loving heavenly Father, who is more than happy to hear your requests, but you can't make demands on Him. You can't tell Him exactly when and how He must answer your prayers.

I think it goes without saying that you cannot ask the Lord for something that is directly against His Word. For example, you cannot pray, "Lord, please can you break up a marriage" or "Lord, please can you make someone marry me!"

Praying like this will get an automatic "no" from the Lord. He will not say "yes" in His Word and then "no" when you pray. On the other hand, He will not say "no" in His Word and then change His mind when you pray.

The Lord will always answer according to His timing and also according to His Word.

4. Break Out of the Rut

Relax a little in your prayer times, especially now that you are going through these teachings. Take it easy. Enjoy this process of intercessory prayer. Play around with it.

Take times in which you bring requests to the Lord. Take times when you only speak what He shows you. Take other times when you do nothing but sit with your guitar or praise Him the whole time.

Praise and sing your prayers out. Enjoy this phase of your prophetic journey. There is no stiff rulebook for prayer that says, "five minutes of tongues, then five minutes of getting revelation, then five minutes of answering requests."

If that were so, I would get so bored. If your times of intercession have become dry and boring, do something different. Break out of the rut.

> **KEY PRINCIPLE**
>
> There are so many different ways you can approach the Lord, but the key in all of them is to pray in faith.

The secret is to put aside your own ideas and to let Him have His way.

There is no rulebook for how to have a conversation with the Lord. Throw it away. Break free. Liberate your times of intercession and you are going to start experiencing new power. Just hand your list over to the Lord and let Him take over.

When you do that, you are going to start praying according to His Word and His will. You are going to start seeing some miracles.

The conclusion to using petitionary prayer? Bring your prayers to the Lord. He loves to hear them - but then be sensitive enough to know when to shut up or when to push through.

Chapter 09

The 3rd Function: Persistent Prayer

Chapter 09 – The 3rd Function: Persistent Prayer

> *Colossians 4:12 Epaphras, who is one of you, a bondservant of Christ, greets you, always laboring fervently for you in prayers, that you may stand perfect and complete in all the will of God.*

It is easy to see the nature of a true intercessor. He is one like Epaphras, who persists fervently in prayer! Bringing it closer to home, if anyone taught me about persistent prayer it was my stepmom.

Perhaps it was so outstanding for me, because I was always so quick to pray once and then move on. Not her though. When she heard that a family member was diagnosed with cancer, she did not leave her prayer closet until the answer came.

When there was a financial crisis or an onslaught of spiritual warfare, you would walk past her bedroom in the early hours of the morning and hear her praying fervently – releasing decrees and calling the natural to bow to the spiritual!

When she first started out in prayer, she did not always see results. Perhaps that is why she sought God so hard on the subject! Over time though, she learned how to keep her fervency, but pray effectively as well! As a result, she saw many miracles on her watch.

Perhaps because I have seen this first hand so much, I am so passionate about the power of persistent prayer. So often as prophets, we pray once or twice, but when the answers do not come, we move on.

Over time you wonder why God did not answer. You wonder why the miracle did not come. When Jesus walked the earth not everyone was healed immediately. Though He was the son of God, even He had to persist at times to see things happen.

Now there was no doubt in Him. He was perfect and most definitely knew how to speak to His mountains! So if Jesus could persist until answers came, how about you? It was not uncommon for Jesus to pray through the night, yet so often when we do not see answers the next day, we become despondent.

THE FERVENT PRAYER

It is the fervent prayer of the just that avails much! (James 5:16) If you have taken time to get into the presence of the Lord and He has told you what to pray, then it is for you to follow through.

It is for you to be like Epaphras, and to labor in prayer on behalf of God's people. It is when you push past your boundaries that you will move to a higher plane in prayer.

MOVE PAST YOUR PLATEAU

We all have limitations, but if you want to see bigger miracles, then you need to stretch past your limitations as well. Jesus was in touch with the Father all the time and as a result, just one word from Him, and the fig tree gave up all life!

Just one word from Jesus, and demons ran away. Eyes were healed. The natural world came into line with the words that He spoke. You can see these kinds of miracles too, if only you persisted in prayer.

The only catch of course, is that the Lord will call you to persist in prayer at the most inconvenient times. This was certainly Jesus' lot in life. He was always called up to the mountain in the middle of the night to pray.

So do not be surprised when the Lord wakes you up in the early hours of the morning to come into the Throne Room. Is this not what happened to Samuel the first time he heard the Lord's voice?

It happened in the night when everyone was asleep. That is why he ran to Eli. Have you ever questioned why the Lord chooses to be so inconvenient sometimes?

Well there are in fact, a number of reasons for this.

The 3rd Function: Persistent Prayer

> **KEY PRINCIPLE**
>
> The first reason that God wakes you up to pray is that this is the only time you are silent enough to hear Him!

When you are running through your day, if you do not take the time to go to the Throne Room, you will often overlook those nudges of the spirit, calling you to action.

You focus so much on your responsibilities, that you override the gentle tugging that is calling you to prayer. So the Holy Spirit has to wait for you to settle down so that you can hear Him better.

CALLED FROM THE SHOWER...

So He will call you to prayer, or try to get your attention when it is quiet. You might find this funny, but I often get these calls in the shower!

Some of the most profound teachings that I ever preached, came to me while I was in the bathtub or shower. After a while of this happening, it finally dawned on me why it happened this way.

It was the only time of day when I was alone and had 5 minutes of silence around me! I could lock the kids out (guilt free) wash away all my struggles for the day and just have a moment to put my mind into neutral.

I can imagine the Lord saying, "Ah ha! Finally! Now I can get a word in!"

And so, my best times with the Lord, usually happens when I do not expect it. The same is for you. The Lord will call you to pray or give you an item to put on your prayer list when He is able to get His message through.

This might happen in the car, in the early hours of the morning, or when you are putting your mind into neutral while on a walk.

No Opposition

The second reason why the Lord wakes you up to pray in the night, is it is the only time when you will not have opposition when you pray! Remember how the angel silenced Zacharias so that he could not speak against the plan that God had?

Well that is the same principle for why God calls you to pray when everyone else is sleeping. You have already learned that words contain power and some of the greatest opposition when we face in prayer is when the words of others are in direct conflict with God's will.

So the Lord will have you pray at a time when others cannot oppose you. During these times, you will find the anointing will flow a lot easier. It is because there is no one awake to send out any words that will contradict what you are praying.

Do you really think that Samuel could have heard the Lord so clearly with Eli looking over his shoulder? No, he needed to be alone and in the quiet to get such a direct word. Even in the Old Testament, you will see how often the Lord spoke to His people at night.

> **KEY PRINCIPLE**
>
> So do not be surprised if you suddenly wake up in the middle of the night and it feels like sleep just left you. If this happens, you are receiving a call to prayer!

EMERGENCY PRAYER – STANDING PROXY

Another reason why the Lord might call you to pray at inconvenient times is not because of your situation, but because of what someone else is going through. I heard so many fantastic testimonies of intercessory prayer growing up.

I heard a story of a woman who was in a car accident. She could not move and could not pray out loud. Inside she was crying out to God! Across town, the Lord raised up an intercessor to pray! They did not know the woman, and did not know why they needed to pray – they just prayed as God led.

That woman was found and rescued from the dangerous situation she was in! Sometimes the Lord will call you to "stand proxy" for someone. In other words, when there is someone that cannot pray, but is crying out to God from within, He will give you the words to pray on their behalf.

In other words, you do not simply pray for the person, you pray as the person!

When this happens, you will likely find yourself praying in tongues more than in your natural language. Often you will find yourself praying for someone that you do not even know, or have never met before. This is intercession in its purest form and certainly the most rewarding experience you will ever have in prayer!

Persistent Prayer – Breaking Ground

When you allow the Lord to inconvenience you, you will break past the plateau in your prayer life. You will be called by the Holy Spirit to pray beyond your circle of contacts. He will use you to pray on behalf of other ministries, people, and nations.

You will indeed learn to "plant and uproot" as a prophet. All of this will take place in your prayer closet.

In all of these case scenarios though, there is one element that is essential - persistence!

The 3rd Function: Persistent Prayer

> **KEY PRINCIPLE**
>
> If you do not pray until the answer comes, you will always fall short of the manifested miracle.

Now sometimes you might feel the call to prayer, but you do not get any revelation, or you do not receive the words to pray. When this happens then you need to follow the direction of this scripture!

> *Romans 8:26 Likewise the Spirit also helps in our weaknesses. For we do not know what we should pray for as we ought, but the Spirit Himself makes intercession for us with groanings which cannot be uttered.*

These "groanings" take place when you allow the Holy Spirit to pray on your behalf. This means to simply pray in tongues. This is very common before any decrees go forth.

I like to call this experience, "Breaking Ground."

BREAKING GROUND

If you look at a piece of land that needs to be prepared for planting, before they can sow seeds and reap a harvest, the field needs to be broken up first. The soil becomes compact and hard during the season. For the seeds to flourish, that soil must be broken up.

Often, if the field has not been used for farming before, it will contain weeds and rocks that have to be removed.

When you "break ground" as an intercessor, that is exactly what you are doing – you are digging out rocks. You are preparing the ground for the decree to be spoken forth.

This is certainly a function of prophetic ministry and any believer can be called of God to pray in this way. There are circumstances that need to come in line for that miracle to manifest.

Not only that, but sometimes when you are standing proxy, you do not get all the revelation for the person you are praying for. Sometimes they might be a complete stranger. Instead of trying to figure it out, just pray fervently in tongues!

Praying as a Team

This is certainly something we experience as a ministry team very often. When the Lord gives us a new direction, before we can even decree it into the earth, He will have us persist in prayer and "break ground" first. Now you can get discouraged when you do not see answers right away.

The worst thing that you can do is to stop! How do you know that the decree was not just about to be released? How do you know that the answer was just around the corner?

As you break ground and pray in the spirit, you are giving the angels license in the earth to arrange the circumstances. You are giving them what they need to "loose what is in heaven to be loosed upon the earth!"

Now you might not have the words in your natural tongue, but that is all right, because the Holy Spirit knows exactly what mountains need to be removed, and what field needs to be ploughed.

All you need to do, is be willing to keep praying and laying the groundwork until the miracle comes. In my personal experience, this is the longest part of the intercessory process. Depending on what God wants to do, this kind of prayer can range from days to months!

MINISTRY FOUNDATION

This kind of prayer lays a ministry foundation! Before you even step out in the call God has given to you, pray it through first! Break the ground and prepare the field for when God starts planting seeds.

This step is essential in intercession, but so many miss out on it. Either they send out empty prayers or they give up when there are no immediate results.

No! Push through! Persist. Drill through that rock and before you know it, the same will happen for you as it did for Moses – water will begin to gush out.

Your fervent prayers will avail much. The more you do it, the more results you will see. The more you do it, the more faith you will have.

Has God been calling you to pray at inconvenient times lately? Hear the call and rise to the occasion! He is answering your prayer to be used of Him!

When you come to prayer, are the words not finding you? Then pray in the spirit. You need to allow the Holy Spirit to intercede through you. Break that ground up until the decree comes and the miracles manifest.

Taking what you have learned so far, you can change the world. So what are you waiting for? Before they can do anything, the angels are waiting on you to pray!

CHAPTER 10

THE 4TH FUNCTION: PROPHETIC WARFARE

Chapter 10 – The 4th Function: Prophetic Warfare

> *Psalms 59:1 Deliver me from my enemies, O my God; defend me from those who rise up against me.*

What is it about us prophets that just bring out the bullies? I am sure that not every prophet is bullied at school, but somehow the fact that I was insecure and weak, seemed to attract bullies to me like bees to honey.

I remember one incident at school when I was circled by a pack of girls, each taking a turn to pull my hair and call me names. I looked around and there was no one to defend me. I was devastated. When I could get away, I ran to the bathroom and huddled in a corner to cry.

At that moment, I felt so alone, even though I knew that the Lord Jesus was there. How I wished there was a champion to come to my defense. Well, as prophets, we may have suffered our own phases of rejection, but they have equipped us to be the defender of the weak.

This in essence, is what it means to engage in spiritual warfare on behalf of others as a prophet. I have an entire book dedicated to the subject of prophetic warfare, so in this chapter I am going to focus on the purpose of warfare in prophetic intercession.

There are times when believers come under attack from the enemy. It is your responsibility as a prophet to rise up as their defender! There are times when the enemy has been given license in someone's life and the Lord will call you to stand on their behalf.

You might be praying when you see someone in the spirit and God knows that you must pray for them. The moment you start praying though, you feel that something is wrong in the spirit. You sense a heaviness or feel that they are in trouble in some way.

When this happens, the Lord is calling you to do warfare on their behalf.

REASONS FOR WARFARE

There are many reasons that the Lord will call you to do spiritual warfare on behalf of others. I remember a time when we were praying for the salvation of someone close to us. That was warfare! The Lord had us come against the bondage that was hindering them.

Not long after that, the Lord arranged the circumstances and that person got saved. I know that it was the warfare we did in the spirit that caused this to come to pass. In moments like these, the following passage comes to life:

> *2 Corinthians 10:4 For the weapons of our warfare are not carnal but mighty in God for pulling down strongholds,*

When you pick up your sword and bind the enemy in the life of another, you are saving them from the bully. The enemy circles God's people like vultures, wearing them down. It is for you to be their defender in the spirit.

How to Engage in Prophetic Warfare

Very often someone will be under an attack that prevents them from hearing what God wants to tell them. So often, when God has called me to do warfare, it was not to pray that someone "gets a revelation" but rather that they can be free from the bondage that is blocking their ears.

Way too often, prophets misunderstand this and end up praying their own burden instead of what God intends. They start praying their own ideas and pray for that person to make the right choices, when in reality, you just need to bind the enemy. Then the voice of the Holy Spirit, which is already talking to them, can be heard.

For example, you might have someone that is in a relationship they should not be in. They are being led astray, and as you come to pray, the Lord brings them to mind.

What Not to Pray

The worst thing you can pray is, "Lord I pray that they break up with this person. I pray that you will make them see things my way."

The 4th Function: Prophetic Warfare

You might be getting the right revelation, but you are applying it incorrectly. You will not see results. Instead, you should be applying the following passage,

> *Ephesians 6:12 For we do not wrestle against flesh and blood, but against principalities, against powers, against the rulers of the darkness of this age, against spiritual hosts of wickedness in the heavenly places.*

1. Bind Demons – Not People

Rather, you should be binding the voice of the enemy that is leading them astray.

Key Principle

> When it comes to spiritual warfare, you do not bind a person – you bind the enemy!

I have seen way too many prophets pray prayers that to put it bluntly, sound more like spiritual witchcraft than true prayers of intercession. If the Lord Himself does not force us to do anything against our will, then how can you force your will on someone?

You cannot bind a person. If you remember this, you can always keep your spiritual warfare on track. I have seen way too many prophets go astray on this little point. I have seen wives, binding someone trying to break up her marriage.

I have seen fathers binding people that are leading their children astray.

It is not the person you should be looking at, but rather what is motivating them. See the enemy for who he really is. He is the bully here. When you see that, you can even see the offender through the eyes of Christ.

In fact, the greatest warfare you can ever do against someone, is to love them! If you want to undo the works of the enemy, then speak forth blessing, and love on those that are persecuting you.

Isn't this what the Word says when it tells us to love our enemies? I love the verse in Psalms that I have used for this chapter. David cries out to God to deliver him from his enemies.

He does not bind his enemies or try to sort them out himself. He asked God for deliverance because he knew where the power lay! The same is true for you.

> **KEY PRINCIPLE**
>
> True power in spiritual warfare does not lie in binding people, but in binding demons.

When you allow this concept to sink in, then you are ready for the Lord to use you to be the defender of His people.

Remember how I shared in the previous chapter that you need to allow the Lord to speak first? Once you have done that, you might receive a vision or revelation that is a call to spiritual warfare. This might happen in a number of ways.

You might see a demon in the spirit. You might feel a knot in your stomach when you are praying for someone.

When this happens, it is time for you to pray it through and also to keep your focus straight.

2. WARFARE MEANS TALKING TO THE DEVIL

Following on from my last point – you are not binding a person, but a demon. This means that you are talking to the devil and telling him to leave. Jesus sure had no problem with this at all.

When confronted with a demon, Jesus did not say, "Um, Father could you please make this demon go away?"

Nope, He looked that person straight in the eye and said, "Come out of him!"

He spoke to the demon and not the person. So when you engage in spiritual warfare, do not make the mistake of praying,

"Lord please can you make this demon go away."

No, you look that demon straight in the eye and pray, "I bind you in Jesus name! You loose your hold on God's child!"

You will find this happening a lot when you bring a petition before the Lord as well. You will bring a need before the Lord and feel the go ahead to start and pray.

When You Hit a Wall

The moment you do that though, you will feel like you just hit a demonic wall in the spirit! When this happens, it is time to take up your sword.

What you are feeling is the conflict that the person is in and you might need to wrestle with that bondage for a while. Once you have bound the enemy, it opens the way for you to decree and speak blessing.

The Lord wants to bless His children and often He has already spoken His will, but the enemy is standing in the way of that will coming to pass.

Praying for Finances

I have often had this when praying concerning finances. I have seen how the Lord has already given the go ahead, but there is a block in the spirit. Do you think that the enemy wants you to be blessed?

Do you really think that satan wants you to prosper and use those finances to advance the Kingdom of

God? It is not God that withholds His blessing from His Children, it is the enemy that does that.

Often, all it takes is for a prophet to bind the work of the enemy, for that blessing to come forth. Believing God for a miracle is the easy part. The Lord does not take long to give an answer, especially when He has clearly declared it in the Word.

It is the enemy that will stand against that. He will send people and circumstances to distract you. He will use every open door he has, to try and circumvent that blessing from coming to you.

The Process God Follows

Praying for finances is definitely a cry of attack in the ears of the enemy! He knows that when the Kingdom of God is blessed, we hold the power to spread the Word of God!

Perhaps what you do not realize though, is that there is a process when you begin to pray for your needs. This is something that I have come to experience so often in my own experience.

The Order for Financial Miracles

The Lord follows an order when He provides. As you begin to intercede, He will start to speak to the hearts of those closest to you. So if you brought your need before the Lord and a close family member knocks on your door, do not reject them!

So often we want to see a big miracle and do not consider a family member providing a need much of a miracle. What you do not realize is that the Lord wants to give those closest to you the first opportunity to be blessed!

As they give to you in faith, they are giving to the Lord Himself! Is this not what this scripture means?

> *Matthew 25:34 Then the King will say to those on His right hand, 'Come, you blessed of My Father, inherit the kingdom prepared for you from the foundation of the world:*
>
> *35 for I was hungry and you gave Me food; I was thirsty and you gave Me drink; I was a stranger and you took Me in;*

If someone close to you sees your suffering, and is moved by the Lord to meet that need, they are not giving to you, but to the Lord. Do not steal that opportunity for blessing from them!

If those close to you cannot answer, or do not want to answer, then the Lord will begin to move further afield to meet your needs. He will move to friends, acquaintances, work opportunities and then finally the world. That is why it takes longer at times.

When there is no one that the Lord can bless by providing through them, He will go further afield and provide through the systems of the world.

1. Using Tongues to Drill Through Rock

That is why in intercession you will often find yourself "drilling through rock." You will start to pray and you know you are praying in the right direction, but feel that wall in your face.

That is the time to break through it to the other side. It is not like you are not getting revelation – rather you feel that the enemy is blocking the path in front of you.

When this happens, the best thing to do is to pray in tongues, like I taught in the previous chapter, until you feel a lift. When you do not know what to pray, then pray in tongues until you feel a release in the spirit.

Very often when I do spiritual warfare like this, I will even hear my tongue change. Then I know that I am standing against something very specific in the spirit.

In our ministry, we have established something we call a "Prayer Wall" taken from the illustration of the walls that Nehemiah built. We describe it as each prophet taking a "piece of their wall" and establishing it until the land is protected.

Well, as a prophet, you are on just one part of that wall, but together we are the defenders of the Body of Christ. This means that it is likely we will all pray something different.

2. One Wars - Another Decrees

I certainly see this in our own ministry. We will often establish 24-hour prayer wall times. Being international it is easy to arrange it around the different time zones. Each one of the prophets takes an hour to pray and decree what God wants them to on behalf of the ministry and the Church.

More often than not, when we start off, those prophets have it tough! They are the ones that feel the "rock" in their face. They pray in tongues. I watch as the prayer reports pour in… for the first few days everyone seems to sing the same song,

"It was tough in the spirit today. I had to do warfare and just pray in tongues until I felt a lift."

Then slowly, a bit at a time, the reports start to change as the breakthrough comes. Suddenly it feels as if every stone is torn down and the heavens open! The revelation flows and the decrees start coming.

> **KEY PRINCIPLE**
>
> So if you keep praying and feel that you are not moving on to the "Decree" phase as we talk about in the next chapter, then it is likely that you need to do some warfare.

What I love about this, especially if you can do it with a group, is that one person will lay the foundation and another will put on the capstone.

As the apostle, the Lord will often give me the decree that needs to be spoken. When this happens though, I know that it is because of the prophets that have been "drilling through rock" for days already.

3. BE ON THE LOOKOUT

You will find the Lord will use you this way very often. It is seldom that I do not engage in spiritual warfare when I pray.

We are after all, the watchmen on the wall! How else will you see the enemy coming if you are not on the lookout?

So not only is it for you to be sensitive to the work of the enemy at play, but it is also for you to be a defender. It is for you to pray until the arrows have been sent back, the babies birthed and the way opened ahead of God's people.

So if you feel as if you are coming against something when you pray, realize that you hold a very important place in the Church. You are the one God needs to defend His people.

He needs you to pray through the attacks that are hindering His perfect plan in the Church, and in the lives of individuals.

So although you might pray for healing, finances, or blessing on a new project, do not be surprised if the first thing, you see, is a demonic bondage.

You see it because the enemy is trying to block the perfect will of God. When you can remove the blockages that the enemy is putting in the way, then the decrees of blessing flow naturally.

If you are not getting a breakthrough or seeing results to your prayer, could it be that you forgot to tell the enemy to "get off your land!"

Now for the most part, I do not need to encourage prophets to do warfare. Having faced their fair share of being bullied, they are only too happy to send the enemy packing.

The important part is to realize that the Lord has given you this place to be a defender of others and not just to take care of your own problems. When the Lord wants to move on this earth, you can be sure the enemy will try to stop it.

4. COUNTERACT SATAN'S AGENTS

With so many willing agents at his side, satan often turns the balances in his favor. It is up to us to make sure that does not happen. The great thing is that it does not take much.

Check out this awesome passage:

> *Deuteronomy 32:30 How could one chase a thousand, and two put ten thousand to flight, unless their Rock had sold them, and the Lord had surrendered them?*

It means that you are a lot stronger than any demon. For any one of a thousand agents that the enemy has, teaching his doctrine, you just need to speak one word of authority and all their work is undone.

Now imagine an army of prophets armed with this kind of authority? The enemy's days are numbered!

I thought to myself once how incredible it would be to have prophets in office doing warfare and sending out decrees 24 hours a day. You have the enemy sending out his words into the earth all around us. No wonder we see the Church stumbling around in the dark.

It does not take much to turn on the light though. When you are praying for a Church, see more than just the pastor that is missing it. See more than the husband that is treating his wife badly or the drug addict that is a bad influence on your child.

Rather see the forces behind that and come against them in the name of Jesus. Reserve your love for the Church. Rather give them your heart and the enemy the sword and not the other way around!

5. KNOW WHEN IT'S TIME TO STOP

There is no greater feeling than the lift that comes after you get a breakthrough in warfare. You feel like the air gets lighter!

You can make the mistake at this point to keep "bashing" the devil and forgetting that your purpose is to speak forth God's will into the earth.

So do not get so caught up in talking to the devil that you forget to speak on behalf of the Lord.

I know... another one of our prophetic weaknesses! I have heard some prophets get so excited about binding the devil that they forget that he is a defeated foe.

All, you need to do, is kick him off your land and then it is time to send out the decrees that take even more land! All you are doing warfare for, is to get that breakthrough.

Once you have the breakthrough, then it is time to speak forth God's word and to make things happen. It is time to give the Lord license so that His plan can come to pass.

> **KEY PRINCIPLE**
>
> So intercessory warfare is simple. You thwart the plans of the enemy and then give the Lord the license instead so that His plan can come into play.

Isn't this what Jesus did?

> *Colossians 2:15 Having disarmed principalities and powers, He made a public spectacle of them, triumphing over them in it.*

After that He resurrected and gave us all authority in His name! He bound the devil when He died and then brought forth the perfect plan of the Father.

This is the model we are to follow. Do enough warfare to get a breakthrough and bind the enemy up. Once you have bound up that "strongman", it is time to decree and speak forth what God wants to do.

If you follow this order, you will feel the anointing increase and you will also get more decrees.

Intercessory warfare should be part and parcel of what you pray as a prophet. Use it effectively and see God move!

Chapter 11

The 5th Function: Prophetic Decree

Chapter 11 – The 5th Function: Prophetic Decree

> *Isaiah 55:11 So shall My word be that goes forth from My mouth; it shall not return to Me void, but it shall accomplish what I please, and it shall prosper in the thing for which I sent it.*

Don't you just hate long-winded, boring teachers that take half an hour just to get to the point? I don't know, maybe it is an expressive thing, but I want the punch line.

I am the same kind of person that doesn't enjoy a joke that goes on and on and on. In my mind, I am thinking, "Let's get to the punch line. Let's get to the good part."

I am the same if I watch a movie. Don't start off too slowly. I want to get to the point of this whole thing. I don't want to feel as if I am sitting around wasting my time.

Well, unfortunately, when it comes to intercession some prophets are like those long-winded teachers. You get the feeling that they are so rusty that need to warm up or something.

So instead of getting to the point, they talk about nothing and they pray these long-winded prayers. They are hoping that somewhere during their prayer that "bam!" something profound will jump out, bringing down the glory cloud!

In the meantime, if you are the poor sucker praying with this person, you have to suffer through...

"Oh Lord, we thank you for your presence here today as we have gathered for a specific purpose to..."

"Father, we just submit ourselves to you, and if it is your will, may our words reach heaven..."

"Lord, we realize that we are not worthy of you Lord to be used by you, Jesus..."

"Thank you, Jesus, Father God, for this appointed time, Jesus, Father God..."

"blah blah blah...!"

Lord deliver me! These are all empty, boring words! Throw them away.

Dump the "Blah Blah"

If you want to take your times of intercession from mediocre to powerful, that's the first thing that you have to trash - all the "blah blah" words that you put into your prayers. They sound terribly spiritual, but they mean nothing.

Some people might think that it sounds good, but the reality is that they are boring and empty. These words are nothing but fluff like cotton candy.

So, then you ask yourself, "Why am I doing it?" It's simple – It is because everybody else is doing it.

Because it is all you have seen, you are putting in these status quo buzzwords to feel like you are in the "in crowd."

I know that the Scripture says that He knows what you are going to pray before you pray it. However, it doesn't mean that we have to put the poor guy through suffering by repeating it again and again… and again! He already got the punch line!

> **KEY PRINCIPLE**
>
> This is the essence of what prophetic decree is all about. It is about cutting through the "blah blah" and getting to the punch line.

I know that the prophet in you is jumping up and down on the inside saying, "Yes! Yes! Let's do it!" So let's look at the rules of engagement for prophetic decree!

INTERCESSOR VS. PROPHET

By now I am sure you see the correlation between your prophetic ministry and intercession. It is true that someone can be an intercessor and not necessarily a prophet.

I will say this though, if you are looking for those who are functioning in prophetic ministry and have the call to rise up into office, you will find them in the local intercessors group! A hunger to pray is one of the signs of a prophetic call.

So while an intercessor is not necessarily a prophet automatically, their hunger for prayer is a sign that they could very well be called to this ministry.

On the other hand, if you are a prophet, intercession is very much a part of your function in the Church. As we dig into the subject of decree, the last pieces will fall into place.

THE POWER OF PROPHETIC DECREE

If you want to make your prayers full of power, it is time that you learn to get to the punch line too. That punch line is called prophetic decree. Until you get to the point where you are speaking decrees - you are just sitting talking to the walls.

Have you ever seen a wall jump up and do something? No, it just carries on standing there. If you are wondering why your prayers are bouncing off the ceiling there, is a very good reason for it – they are!

When you speak a decree under the anointing of the Holy Spirit, those words don't bounce. Instead, they go out like a sword into the earth and they do not return void - rather they accomplish that for which they were sent.

Now, if you don't have the "accomplish that for which they were sent" dynamic happening in your prayer times, then you are just playing with bouncing balls.

Do you remember those fun bouncy balls that we got as kids? I loved them. You would bounce them and they flew into the air bouncing all over the place.

Well, that is a good picture of those boring, empty, cotton-candy words that are prayed. They are just bouncing all over the place and irritating everyone.

If you are praying for somebody else, please have pity on them. They don't want to suffer through your boring dialog either.

Come on, you know the guys I am talking about. You get an intercessor group together and there is bound to be at least one of them. Someone that likes the sound of their own voice and goes on and on and on, until you think, "Oh Lord, are you as bored as I am?" Yes, I think He is because He doesn't answer those prayers. They don't move Him.

People think that the "many words" of the fervent prayer avail much. No! It is the faith that is going to move the hand of God. Don't think that you are going to talk Him into submission.

1. Choose Words of Authority

You can say three words to change the world. That is what Jesus did on that cross. With just three simple words, "It is finished!" the ground shook and the veil of the temple was torn. The whole earth went into travail over just three words.

What a stark contrast that is to someone blabbing and blabbing at God and not seeing any results.

Prophet of God, it is time to change some tactics. It is time to speak forth the kind of words that bring power.

Just take a look at Jesus' ministry. When it came to teaching He was thorough and He covered a lot of subjects. However, when it came to performing healing or speaking into somebody's life we get,

"He who has no sin, cast the first stone."

He didn't give them the whole dialog. One sentence so powerful that they all turned around and left.

In fact, sometimes He didn't even have to say a word. They tried to push Him off the hill and He just looked at them and walked through. That's authority. That's power.

That same authority and power are available to you if you can just learn to tap into it.

> **KEY PRINCIPLE**
>
> There is a power that the prophet has to speak things into existence.

You will see this often in the Old Testament.

> *Isaiah 9:6 For unto us a Child is born, unto us a Son is given; and the government will be upon His shoulder. And His name will be called Wonderful, Counselor, Mighty God, Everlasting Father, Prince of Peace.*

Isaiah was doing a lot more here than just saying, "A little bit of news for your interest guys, one day a son will be born…" Rather, he was saying, "It shall be! A son will most certainly be born – I release that!"

He does not say, "Unto us a child will be given…" He says rather, "Unto us a child is given…" In other words, this is God's plan and it is set in stone. Isaiah was releasing that reality into the earth, as will you when you allow God to use you effectively.

Their very words caused the plan of God to be formed in the earth.

You see, when the prophet says in the Old Testament, "There shall be…" he wasn't just predicting, he was decreeing.

When the Lord was saying, "Let there be light." He wasn't saying, "Gee, I hope there will be light." He was not just predicting that that light would show up one day. No, He was speaking it forth. He was creating with His very words, "Let there be." And there was.

2. Decree Releases Creative Force

Isaiah said, "A child will be born, a son will be given, a government will be upon his shoulders." These weren't just idle and fluffy words. These were words of power. They went into the creation, took hold of the creation and caused things to come to pass.

Imagine it for a moment. Imagine that the words you speak go into the earth, and take hold of the creation by force just like the words of Jesus did, to create a reaction.

Then when you are praying for finances or the Church, you are not just talking, but those words are living and powerful. Those words go out and grab hold of the circumstances and transform them to come into line with the Word of God.

That's what being a prophet is about! That's intercession! Without that power, you haven't even begun to understand prophetic ministry. You haven't even begun to understand what it means to be a prophet.

So, God gave you a couple of visions... so what? You got a couple of words of knowledge, a couple of words of wisdom. Good for you! So can every other believer.

What sets you apart is your ability to speak forth prophetic decree. If you are leaving out one of the most important aspects of the prophetic calling, you haven't even begun to fulfill your prophetic mandate.

Chapter 11

WHAT MAKES THE PROPHET COUNT

Don't you realize the power that is in your mouth? That is why it is so important to get into His Throne Room and get revelation. You are going to find that these words will not come when you are standing in front of the crowd looking good.

I am the kind of prophet that if I am going to take the time to speak the word of God, can it please be a word that I don't have to repeat?

I can imagine that this is how God feels. "You know, I have got so much to do. I have the whole universe to take care of. When I speak forth a word, can it go forth and accomplish that for which I have sent it, so that I don't have to keep sending it out again and again?"

That would most certainly be my take on Isaiah 55:11 that I put at the beginning of this chapter. When you decree as a prophet, those words should not return void.

3. PRAY IN FAITH

Now how are you going to get to that point? You are going to get to that point by praying in faith - by putting aside all your flapping lips and idle words. Speak what God wants you to say, and when He wants you to say it, with the authority of the prophet.

You see, now you are starting to see the difference between a believer flowing in the gifts, and a prophet who stands in office.

> **KEY PRINCIPLE**
>
> When a prophet stands in office and they decree with authority, what they speak forth comes to pass.

I can't begin to tell how many times I have spoken words like this over people's lives. When I do, I don't care whether they like it or whether they receive it. It is not about that at all. I could have spoken it at home in my closet. They don't even need to hear it and I know it is coming to pass.

Just sometimes it is nice for them to hear it, so they know what is going on. You know, if they suddenly come up against a wall they know, "Ah, Colette Toach released me into training that's why this is happening."

That is why I emphasized making sure you hear from God first and why the previous book was all about learning to hear His voice. When you know that you have heard from God and then feel the anointing, you will also pray in faith. This is where things start to happen.

4. Speak With Authority

You will learn that it is not about how eloquent you are, but how full of power you are. The point is not what sounded nice, but rather that you spoke with authority.

Decree is not, "This is a general word for you that you can decide to keep or reject."

Decree is a creative word. It carries with it a creative power to cause those things that are not, as though they were! (Rom 4:17)

I am sure as you read this, you can already identify what I am talking about. You hear a prophetic word and you think, "Ah that's a nice little word." Then you have others who speak a word and you would not label it as "nice". Rather it is "Wow! That's God." You sense the authority and awe of the Holy Spirit on it. That is what is available to you.

BEST PLACE TO PRACTICE

The best place to practice this, is in your prayer closet. Don't think that you are going to stand as a hotshot and do this now in front of the Church. You will find very few decrees happening there because you will be distracted. You will be distracted by all the other revelation that God needs you to share to minister to His people.

You will find that the word comes when it is quiet. You are like the watchman that sits on the wall at night, waiting while everybody else is sleeping. That is when you are going to get your word.

5. WAIT ON GOD FOR DECREE

So wait on God for the right word and then when the word comes - speak it. It is very simple. Intercession gets you to a place where you can wait on God for that word.

When you are in His Throne Room, make yourself available. Don't think that God will come, knock down your door, and slap you in the face so that you can speak a decree.

You need to make yourself available first. He will certainly try to get your attention, but it is for you to get into His Throne Room and to wait on Him.

Now you will not get a decree every time that you intercede. It is for Him to give them to you. Wait on Him, and when they come, speak them forth.

You see that is the importance of waiting on God. There is no such thing as a "drive-by-intercession".

You need to take time to wait and to listen. That is why you have to stop with all the "flapping-lip" stuff. Stop with all the talking for one minute, so that He can speak.

6. Learn to Listen

Whenever you are too busy jumping to your own conclusions, speaking whatever you want to speak, then God is not going to have a chance to say anything, is He? So learn to listen during your times of intercession. Learn to have times of silence so that you can wait on Him.

> **KEY PRINCIPLE**
>
> Wait for the dove to come. Don't feel rushed or pushed.

Rushing into intercession is a terrible mistake, especially if you are interceding in a group. You feel rushed, "Okay, the Lord spoke, let's go home." Take time to wait on Him!

"Oh, it is late. Let's have a quick prayer time. I have to go to take care of the kids. I have to take the car to the shop. Let's quickly pray and run."

You are not going to get decrees. You are not going to enter into this high level of prayer. Let me tell you, it is worth the wait.

7. You Can Always Speak Blessing

There are times when you are going to wait on God and you are not going to get revelation. When this happens, take a word of counsel from me. You can never go wrong speaking blessing.

Don't swing the pendulum here and go from speaking too much to not saying anything at all. It is not fun at all to pray in a group and everybody sits there staring at each other and nobody wants to speak. It is horrible.

You ask them, "Guys, why aren't you praying." They all answer, "Well, because I didn't get revelation."

Now we have to try to get them out of this bad habit. It is such a prophetic thing, isn't it? From one extreme to the next.

First you have to try and shut them up so God can speak and then everybody gets so super-duper spiritual that they don't even want to say amen without getting a vision.

> **KEY PRINCIPLE**
>
> If you come to pray and no one gets revelation, there is nothing wrong with speaking blessing.

We have authority as prophets, even as believers, to release the blessing of God into this earth and to stand on the Word.

So, you have had a good time of intercession, but now it is quiet and you want to cover a bit more ground. At a time like this, there is nothing wrong with saying "Lord, I just want to speak blessing on my sister… "

Perhaps while you are praying, somebody comes to your mind. You do not know why you see them, but you can pray, "I just speak blessing on them, and I speak blessing on everybody here."

You would be surprised, when you start doing that how you tap into something fresh and more revelation flows. Suddenly somebody else will jump in and the ball will be rolling again!

Find Balance

It is all about balance. You know how I always speak about the prophets swinging the pendulum? Even in your times of intercession, you need to learn to come into balance.

On the one hand, you should not be extreme and babbling the Lord to death. On the other hand, do not be so quiet that nobody says anything for an hour because they are all too afraid to pray anything without any revelation.

Find this balance and you can teach it to others. You hold the power of God on your tongue. Use all the functions of prophetic intercession and start seeing real results.

That is, after all, what we want isn't it? To see a change in the Church, and for God to use us to bring it!

PART 03

PROPHETIC MUSIC

Part 03 – Prophetic Music

It is a fact that even from the womb, a child is affected by the sound of music. The sound of our heartbeat echoes a sound of rhythm through our being.

When I learned to play drums, I learned something very interesting regarding what base drum beat to use. I was taught that the base drum mimics our heartbeat and if I played it correctly, I could use it to influence the mood of my listener.

So if I wanted to bring the audience down to a pace for worship, I could mimic the slow steady thud of a heartbeat. If I wanted to raise emotions, then a quick, repetitive pace was in order.

Think about it in your own experience. A song comes on the radio with a fast, paced rhythm and you cannot help but tap your feet. If you are driving and a song begins to play with the gentle melody of a violin and a slow paced rhythm - you start to relax and drive slower.

There is something about music that has a power over our body and soul! It is no surprise then, that when you add the anointing to the natural power of music, that you hold the key to imparting something amazing to God's people.

You have learned about the prophetic anointing and how it has the power to change lives. Well, when you combine the God-given power that music already has on us and then you add the anointing, you can well imagine the impact it will have on God's people.

So why does music hold such a power over us anyway? Well that is what we are going to look at in the first chapter of this section. From there, I will teach you to combine the anointing that God has given to you, with the existing principles of music, to weave together a powerful thread of prophetic music.

As prophets, God has given us the anointing to heal the hearts of His people. He has given us the anointing to usher in the sweet presence of Jesus to help them discover who they are in Him. Regardless of your musical skill, you can learn to flow in prophetic music and so begin to fulfill your function as a prophet in the Church!

CHAPTER 12

THE ORIGIN OF MUSIC

Chapter 12 – The Origin of Music

When you consider that a third of the angels that God created, are worship angels, you start to get an idea of how much music means to the Lord. Isn't it also something to ponder that satan himself, was the leader of the worship angels before he decided to take all the glory for himself!

> *Isaiah 14:11 Your pomp is brought down to Sheol, and the sound of your stringed instruments; the maggot is spread under you, and worms cover you.'*
>
> *12 "How you are fallen from heaven, O Lucifer, son of the morning! How you are cut down to the ground, you who weakened the nations!*
>
> *13 For you have said in your heart: I will ascend into heaven, I will exalt my throne above the stars of God; I will also sit on the mount of the congregation on the farthest sides of the north;*
>
> *14 I will ascend above the heights of the clouds, I will be like the Most High."*

I guess satan felt he had so much influence being the chief musician, that he tried to take some of that glory for himself. Nothing much has changed. Even today, you see how much the enemy uses music to shape the way people think.

ROCKING WITH THE 80'S

When I was trying my hand at running as far from the Lord as I possibly could, I found myself wrapped up in the heavy metal culture. It was here that I met my husband Craig, who was one of the "80's rockers" of our time.

It was a clique, that I came to realize in later years, that was quite universal. We prided ourselves on being metal heads, as if being part of this group gave us a sense of identity.

There were many facets to this archetype, but at the core of it, was the music we listened to. It brought us together from all walks of life. In many ways it became a religion of its own. Looking back, I am amazed at the power that the music had.

The enemy used it to bring people together, give them a common cause (of rebellion - as was ours) and brought with it, a power to cause us to conform. Oh yes, just in case you think the enemy is not smart, think again. He has been using the power of music to manipulate people since the day he was cast out of heaven.

A LAW OF THE SPIRIT

He simply took the existing power of music and added his message to it. Now, just because the enemy has been using this spiritual law for his own means, does not mean we throw the baby out with the bathwater.

Just because he used it to a bad end, does not mean we do not use it at all.

Rather, we need to set our own trend as believers and certainly as prophets! What if we had a "spirit-filled" musical archetype? What if we created our own blend of music that brought people into the presence of the Lord, instead of inciting them to take on the spirit of the world?

Well that is certainly what God has been doing in these last 10 years in the Christian music arena. More and more, you are seeing prophets rising up with a new message. Even with this though, I see a mistake that we need to correct as prophets.

WE ARE NOT OF THIS WORLD

While it is true that music has power, it does not mean that we need to conform to the trends of the world to make use of it. When I read of Christian bands whose inspiration is a worldly one – I wonder what spirit they are ministering with.

> **KEY PRINCIPLE**
>
> How can you minister forth the power of Christ while partaking of the spirit of the world?

No, it is time for a new anointing and music trend – one that finds believers as the forerunners.

It is time that we stop imitating and start originating. It is time that we stop comparing ourselves to the world and be brave enough to come up with something that is uniquely our own.

I have a problem with Christian bands being compared to worldly ones. The prophet in me says, "Shouldn't the worldly bands be compared to us?"

TALENT VS. ANOINTING

We have gone so far as to appointing the most talented musicians as our worship leaders in the church – instead of the most anointed ones! The worship band has to pass through the same stringent testing of skill, as any worldly band.

What happened to us as a Church that someone with a good voice, is chosen over someone that is born again and anointed?

We have unsaved homosexuals playing the piano for worship, unsaved singers leading the praise, and un-anointed (but talented) guitarists "ripping it up" to the flashing of stage lights and a smoke screen.

All in the name of "reaching the generation of today." It is all done in the name of "Giving people something that will make Church attractive."

Perhaps I am old fashioned, but the last time I checked, it was Christ that made the Church attractive. So yes, we are packing butts into the seats. They get to listen to a watered down message and tap their foot to a beat while listening to a moral melody.

All along I am wondering, "Where is the power of Christ?" Yes, the smoke machines sure attract the crowds – but what spiritual condition is that crowd in?

Are they on fire for Christ? Do they even know who Christ is? When the lights dim and the smoke lifts, where is the Holy Spirit?

Where is the Change?

Why aren't divorce rates dropping or abortions being done away with? Where is the power? Where is Christ? Where is the prophetic anointing in the Church?

That is why God is raising up His prophets in this day and age. It is time to stand up and be counted. To be loud enough, proud enough, and full of fire enough to make a difference.

Sure, we are not going to pack the pews with thousands of lukewarm believers who wear a Christian badge on their shoulders. Instead, we will start to raise up a sleeping giant from the remnant that has a true heart for God.

We will have a mighty warrior that is ready to be equipped. Have you become frustrated because those you are trying to reach just do not want what you have? Perhaps you are trying to reach the wrong people!

Perhaps it is time to look for the hidden remnant that has a fire for God, and is ready to shake this world in the name of Christ.

The mega-churches serve their purpose and while they tiptoe carefully around the deeper doctrines of the Word and somehow manage to water down a watered-down message, we as prophets, can use what God has given to us.

> **KEY PRINCIPLE**
>
> In amongst the thousands warming seats, are those who have been given a heart for God. These are the few you are reaching.

There are hot coals that will be able to get the fire going. Revive a few of those coals, and perhaps the dead wood around them will be set on fire as well.

DO NOT BE DISCOURAGED

So do not be discouraged if you feel, as a prophet, that you are alone in your passion. Do not get discouraged if you get ignored. Keep reaching out until you find that "on-fire few." Ignite them, and minister to them. Then watch as they ignite the others around them as well.

As prophets, we can only use what God has given to us. So let us start there. Pick up the anointing that was given to you, combine it with the power of music, and from there - start a fire in the Church!

THE ORIGIN OF MUSIC

> *Job 38:4 Where were you when I laid the foundations of the earth? Tell Me, if you have understanding.*
>
> *5 Who determined its measurements?*
>
> *Surely you know! Or who stretched the line upon it?*
>
> *6 To what were its foundations fastened? Or who laid its cornerstone,*
>
> *7 When the morning stars sang together, and all the sons of God shouted for joy?*

Music has been part of God's plan since the beginning. In fact, it lies at the core of our very creation.

Did you know that as the Lord was creating the earth, that He did it to background music? As He raised His hand to create the beauty we see around us today, the worship angels were singing.

Just imagining this, transports me to the core of what created us. I see the waters over the earth as God faced all that was "without form and void." Then through the skies a sound begins to thunder – the sound of the morning stars. Singing their praise to the Lord and giving Him glory.

MUSIC IN CREATION

Through that, thunders the voice of the Father as He takes the blueprint in His mind, and expresses each line of it through words, saying, "Let there be…"

Listen! There is music in the creation all around us. Close your eyes and listen to the whisper in the trees, and the steady flow of water as it bubbles in a brook.

Listen to the trembling roar of the lion, and steady breathing of a baby sleeping. In each soft moan of the wind, you hear the sound of those morning stars all over again. Music is encoded into creation. It is the building block of what we see all around us.

MUSIC IN OUR BODIES

When I was pregnant, I purchased a little monitor that would allow me to hear my baby's heartbeat in the womb. Have you ever laid your ears on the belly of a pregnant woman?

There is so much going on in there. From the steady thud of her heartbeat to her various organs sounding out, everything is in natural harmony. You can hear an entire orchestra of sound in there.

Craig and I used to joke and say, God must have created rock music, because listening to how loud that sound was in my belly, we could imagine that a baby is subjected to a lot of noise in the womb. That blend of sounds was reminiscent of some hard-core rock music!

In every moment of that child's day, it hears the steady sound of his mother's heartbeat. As I watched my children grow, the moment that they could sit or stand, they would also dance. I did not teach them. It was natural.

BORN AND BRED TO WORSHIP

I was delighted the first time my eldest daughter finally pulled herself to a standing position. I was even more delighted when I saw her bounce her diapered little behind, to the sound of the song I was playing on my stereo.

Music was just in her! Each child after her was exactly the same – with the exception of my youngest daughter Ruby. She started way earlier than that! Music was her life. I guess being born a day after a seminar, where I played the drums and sang, had that effect on her.

Before she even worded "mama" or "dada" she would sing melodies in her crib. Now right into her teen years, you can always tell when she is near. Melody is always on her lips!

> **KEY PRINCIPLE**
>
> Who puts this desire in our hearts? Who sat a baby down and told it to enjoy music? No one had to – it is something that the Lord put into our very DNA!

It is a resonant force that inspires and propels us forward. It brings our minds to memories past, and is integral in forming the memories of today. I can still remember my wedding day and the song that was sung. It's melody transports me back to a fresh-faced couple, ready to take on the world, but knowing nothing about what awaited them.

In the chapters ahead, I am going to teach you more about what makes music so powerful. From there, I will help you, as a prophet, to develop and use this powerful tool to change the church.

You have yet to experience and see the things that God is about to do through you. There is a reason you are anointed to worship. From this page onwards, the anointing for music and worship will rise up from within you. Take it! Nurture it! Fulfill this powerful function of the prophet.

CHAPTER 13

FINDING THE RIGHT FREQUENCY

Chapter 13 – Finding The Right Frequency

It is a known fact, that scientists can determine the frequency of every object on earth. What is a frequency? Simply put (without getting too technical) frequency is the rate at which something vibrates.

Everything you see in this world has a frequency! Our human ears can only hear up to a certain frequency though. So we can hear the sound of a baby's cry, and the alarm yelling at us, saying that it is time to get up.

Dogs on the other hand, can hear a higher frequency and choose to let you know all about it when they bark up a storm at 4 in the morning! All it takes is a car alarm going off a few miles down the road, and all the dogs in the neighborhood join in!

When you understand this concept, you can only but stand in awe of our mighty God!

> **Key Principle**
>
> There is music all around us! There is a hum at levels we can and cannot hear that all testify of the Lord.

Jesus said,

> *Luke 19:40 But He answered and said to them, "I tell you that if these should keep silent, the stones would immediately cry out."*

Jesus knew that creation had a voice with which it worshipped the Lord.

> *Psalms 89:5 And the heavens will praise Your wonders, O Lord; your faithfulness also in the assembly of the saints.*

The very spirit of God is in the frequency all about us. Unfortunately, it is not just the Lord that uses this frequency for His good purpose.

CONTAMINATED OBJECTS

Having full knowledge of this power, satan has used this for generations to lead people astray. Understanding that objects can contain an evil spirit is a study for somewhere else, but I am going to mention it here, because of how it relates to music specifically.

If the enemy is able to "anoint" objects and people with something demonic, then it also stands to reason that he adds his own "spiritual frequency" to music as well.

How come you can listen to a song and feel oppression on it? The enemy has added his own spiritual frequency, to the existing power of music to get his message out.

That is why it is so important that we get the right frequency ringing through the Church as prophets. How can an unbeliever, under oppression, sing the praises of God?

How can someone, who is not even born-again by the spirit of God, minister to the spirit of God's people? Instead, what he is releasing is the work of the enemy to bring death and to cool the flames of passionate belief.

THE RIGHT FREQUENCY

You already know that the Lord has given you an anointing as a prophet. What you might not realize is that you already have the "right frequency" with which to bring change. All you need to do now, is add music to it, and you have a recipe to ignite hearts and change lives.

THE POWER OF MUSIC

I do not need to prove to you that music has an effect on us, but how about we look at the power it has when combined with the anointing?

> *Acts 16:25 But at midnight Paul and Silas were praying and singing hymns to God, and the prisoners were listening to them.*
>
> *26 Suddenly there was a great earthquake, so that the foundations of the prison were shaken; and immediately all the doors were opened and everyone's chains were loosed.*

As a preacher said once, "Paul and Silas started praising the Lord and He enjoyed it so much, He just started tapping His feet!"

That praise had the power to bring down the prison! When was the last time that the ground shook when you praised God?

Music has a power over our souls, but it also has a power over creation. When you add the "right frequency," that power will be felt physically, as well as emotionally. In fact, it goes even deeper than that.

When you worship with that frequency, the music is felt in the person's spirit, soul, and body!

Music Opens a Door to the Spirit

This was certainly true for my husband Craig when he got born again. As my Dad picked up the guitar and played his simple songs, Craig felt the Lord all over! It opened the door of his spirit, and called him to salvation!

Do not underestimate the power of music! It does a lot more than just stir your emotions – it also has the power to open a door to your spirit.

That is because music causes your spirit, soul and body to unite. Think about it for a moment.

Spirit, Soul and Body

When you read a book, your mind is engaged. At most you will engage your mind, emotions, and will. The only thing your body is doing is holding the book.

This is not so for music – everything is engaged. Not only is your soul (mind, emotions, and will) engaged, but to worship, you need to engage your body as well! You need to open your mouth and sing! You lift your hands in worship.

So there we have it – two out of three so far. Both body and soul are engaged! It goes even further though, because when you sing words, you engage your spirit.

This is because words are spiritual. A dog cannot speak words. There is no such thing as a "dog language." That is because dogs do not have a spirit, only a soul. Humans however, are given a spirit. They speak words and these words are derived from our spirits.

> **Key Principle**
>
> Words and actions release what is inside of your spirit.

Words come directly from our spirits. So there we have it, your spirit, soul, and body are fully engaged when you worship the Lord.

Hopefully you are worshipping the Lord, because you are just as engaged if the worship you are doing is to the latest worldly music band.

THE SPIRIT BEHIND THE MUSIC

Say then you are fully engaged in singing, jumping, and getting your emotions all stirred up at a worldly concert? What spiritual frequency are you allowing into your spirit?

Consider the combination of the singers and the people around you. If everyone there is in the same spirit, with a little bit of "spirit" added on top from the enemy - what are you taking in?

Remember how I taught you in a previous chapter on the anointing, how powerful the corporate anointing is?

It is quite something when we unite our hearts in the same spirit. When we do it in worship to the Lord, we create a thunderstorm! However, what if you are doing it at a concert of unbelievers?

What exactly are you uniting your spirit with? What "corporate anointing" are you tapping into then? Like it or not, when you engage your spirit, soul, and body in anything, you are opening a door to your spirit.

This is a powerful tool when done under the anointing of the Holy Spirit – not so smart when engaging in the spirit of the world.

MUSIC CHANGES CREATION

Now when you add the anointing to that, you have in your hands the ability to change the creation around you! Don't believe me? Well ask Jehoshaphat then what happened when he decided to use worship as a weapon!

In 2 Chronicles 20, they sent the singers ahead of the battle to worship the Lord. As they did this, the Lord fought on their behalf so that the enemy turned around and destroyed one another!

When the children of Israel shouted and blew their trumpets on their last march around Jericho, the walls fell down. When Solomon dedicated the temple, as the people worshipped, a cloud came down and the priests could not stand to minister!

When you worship with all of your being, and the Holy Spirit has anointed you, you have the capacity to bring physical change on the creation!

This is certainly true of how the Lord created the earth – how much more to maintain it? When you use music to pray, intercede, and minister, you are able to bring real change to a real creation!

Can you see then, why the Lord has given you such a special ability? The ability to release the anointing through music! Now not everyone who is a prophet is born knowing how to sing or play a musical instrument.

However, as a prophet, it is important to take hold of this tool and to use it to the best of your ability.

> **KEY PRINCIPLE**
>
> I am not telling you to become talented - I am telling you to become a worshipper!

In the chapters that follow, I am going to teach you a little more on how to release that anointing practically. I will share from my own experience. In that, I pray that you have some new experiences of your own as well.

CHAPTER 14

THE GENTLE BREEZE OF JESUS

Chapter 14 – The Gentle Breeze of Jesus

Craig and I had been living in Mexico for just under a year. We came to a point in our lives where the financial support that we were receiving, from a businessman who had supported us in the work, stopped.

From one month to the other, we went from getting a full salary to getting absolutely nothing.

This was challenging in itself, but let me just put you in the picture. We were 3 families living together at that time, with Craig and I having two daughters. Here we were, sitting in Mexico, which is so far away from South Africa that even the seasons are at different times of the year.

We didn't know the language, we didn't know the people, and we didn't know the food. It took us a month just to learn where to find tea!

Here we were in this foreign land. The visas we had at the time, prohibited us from working. So what were we going to do? We had absolutely no money, and we had nothing but our online presence at the time. What were we going to do for finances?

PROPHETIC MUSIC ROCKS!

So we went on one of our famous beach walks, and it is there that God gave us the revelation.

We were in a desperate situation. We were at our lowest point and didn't know what to do. God didn't open the way for us to leave. We didn't know anybody, and we didn't have anything.

I piped up, "You know what, why don't we take all the materials that we have, put them together and make a prophetic school?"

This, in essence, was the birth of our very first prophetic school, in February 1999.

All we had was a fire in our hearts, a couple of materials that we had preached, and a video camera.

When we got up in the mornings – we didn't really have much to do because at that time the ministry was still very small.

We could get our work out of the way very quickly. There wasn't any food in the house for us to cook a big meal anyway. So what else was there to do?

We had two choices: we were either going to wallow and feel sorry for ourselves because there wasn't any food, or we were going to do the only thing we knew to do – get into His presence.

Chapter 14

PRAISE FOR LUNCH AND DINNER

So we spent the time praising the Lord and learning the principles I am sharing with you here.

We literally ate, slept, and lived music. We would get up in the morning, and if there was tea, we would drink tea. Then we would worship and praise and get into His presence.

We would sing in the spirit, because after a while we got so sick of the songs we knew, that we couldn't bear to hear them anymore.

So instead of singing English songs, we would start singing in the spirit. We could go on for hours, stop for a break, and then worship again.

It was not long before we started to see the fruit of our spiritual investment. It started with little things at first. The first little miracle – someone gave us $50.

For the longest time we lived on $50 a week. Our landlord gave us miraculous favor with our inability to pay rent.

When the money needed to be there though, it was. Our miracles started small – a $50 check feeding 10 people, for a week.

We started to birth something in the spirit - what is now known as Apostolic Movement International. It was this season that birthed and established this ministry.

THE GENTLE BREEZE OF JESUS

The main miracle that took place, was not just with our finances. Something unprecedented started to take place. We became so accustomed to the power and the presence of God during these times of praise and worship.

We would get together in His presence, we would worship, and His cloud would come down. We would sit in His presence, and He would bring healing and reveal things to us.

Jesus was so real. We didn't care if there was nothing else to do. We didn't have TV, and we didn't have any other entertainment. We couldn't even afford to go out. So Jesus was our entertainment.

Something started to happen. We only started realizing this when God started opening the way for people to visit us.

From having nothing, we saw the birth of our first ministry center in Mexico. At our first meeting, we did what was so natural to us. We picked up our guitars, got on the drums, and we started to worship... God started to move.

Something started to happen and people just started to cry in the presence of the Lord. Jesus would reveal Himself to them.

I am not talking about a noisy manifestation or a thundering waterfall. I am talking about a gentle breeze, like when you watch a meadow and you see the wind blow over the grass.

THE RIPPLE EFFECT

The anointing moved over the people like a ripple on a very still lake. It was a physical, very real, effect on the people that came. One by one, they melted in the Lord's presence. The veils were stripped and they came face-to-face with Jesus.

Because of its sweet nature, we called this, "The Gentle Breeze of Jesus".

> **KEY PRINCIPLE**
>
> The Lord explained it to us like this. He said that if there is one thing in this world that satan cannot comprehend - It is love.

The enemy can understand warfare and so many other things, but he cannot understand the love of the Lord. Love and light are powerful - the Scripture says that he cannot comprehend it.

> *John 1:5 And the light shineth in darkness; and the darkness comprehended it not. (KJV)*

TOUCHING PEOPLE'S LIVES

One time we had an opportunity to have a conference at a church in Switzerland. Just beforehand, we stayed on a little farm out in the middle of nowhere. It was a really special time.

This farmer and his wife had set up a guesthouse using their main farmhouse.

Of course, I couldn't live without my guitar, and so we brought it along. When the wife saw our guitar she said, "Oh, you play music?" I answered, "Yes, we sing and worship - we are Christians." She said, "Oh, we love music. I tell you what. I am having a bunch of friends around tomorrow. Could you play some music for us?"

We answered, "Sure." Nobody understood all our English songs. It turned out that she had quite a few friends and they packed their lounge full. I sat there and thought, "Okay Lord, the farm wife only speaks broken English and nobody speaks a word of it... how am I even going to minister to these people?" I was a bit nervous.

The Lord answered, "You just do what you do, and I will do what I do." There were three of us at the time, and we just did what we always did. I got on the guitar, we praised, and worshipped Him, and got into His presence, ignoring everybody there. We just brought the presence of the Lord into that place.

After some time, I looked up and saw all these people watching us with tears flowing down their cheeks. None of these people were believers.

I have so wished that I could have shared more with them, but we didn't understand each other.

Once we had ended, a woman came up to thank us. Between her two words of English and my few words of German she shared, "I didn't understand the songs. The only word that I understood was… Jesus."

This is what you are called to bring to the Church as a prophet – Jesus. To bring everyone to a reality of His love.

Your Mandate Is to Bring His Love

That's your mandate. When you pick up the anointing that He has given to you, take hold of it, and stand up with your music, you are going to release and reveal Jesus.

> **Key Principle**
>
> It is His love that breaks the yoke. It is love that overcomes fear. It is love that brought our Savior down to die for us in the first place.

It is love that is going to revive, restore, and turn His Church around. It is love that is going to make the Bride without spot or wrinkle.

It is love that is going to heal hearts. It is love that is going to heal sickness and disease. It is love that is going to raise the dead, and it is love that God is calling you to breathe upon His Church to revive it.

It is for you to remind the Church why it is so separate from the world. That is your call as a prophet, and it is the power that God has given you.

Music In the Right Place

If you are ever going to use music, it is not for glory, not for fame, and it is not to look wonderful. It is to take that power and anointing, and use it to release His love into His Church.

So fill yourself with it. Breathe it in. Get in His presence and let His love fill you. Let it convict you. Let it cut you to the heart.

Let it put you on your face before Him and say, "Lord, I am not worthy. Forgive my bitterness. Forgive me for thinking that I am so grand that I stood as judge. Oh Lord, I have got so much to say. I got such a big mouth. Let's fill up that big mouth with a big love."

Allow the Holy Spirit to cut you to the heart. Humble yourself before Him and He will lift you up in the sight of man.

Chapter 14

The Price We Pay

Are you prepared to pay the price? Are you prepared to submit to His hand and be cut to the heart? If you want this anointing, power, and authority, I am afraid it comes with a price.

Do you want it badly enough? Then be prepared to pay the price. Be prepared to give up your bitterness, your space, your control, your say, your opinion and what you think.

If you really knew the love of Jesus, you would know that the greatest way to bring a grown man to his knees is not with a hammer, but with the gentle breeze of Jesus.

It is going to be the love of the Lord that will melt him to his knees, and will break through his defenses.

No human being in this world has a defense against this love, because satan doesn't comprehend it. You say, "I am trying to love." No, I am not talking about your ability to love, but I am talking about a supernatural anointing here.

Doesn't it burn in you? When you see the possibilities of what God can and is doing in His Church, doesn't it burn in you to be part of that? When I look at what the Lord has given us, is it even a price anymore? To be so saturated with His love, His presence, and His glory so that it shines from us?

It was love that sent Jesus to the cross. It was because of love that He died, and it was because of love that He has called you. It is because of love that we pay the price.

I want you to submit yourself to the Lord, and I want you to give Him all your "yes... buts". Let it go.

"Yes Lord... but it is not fair."

"I never said it was fair." Life's not fair.

> **KEY PRINCIPLE**
>
> If you want to walk this road, it is a love walk or it is no walk.

Imagine for a moment, the gentle breeze of Jesus sweeping over the Church. See hearts healed and believers becoming strong in their authority. You are called to do that. You are called to put a sword in the hand of the sleeping giant.

The price you pay today will be the fruit that the Church eats tomorrow. That is our inheritance to the Church. May the Lord Jesus find us worthy and continue to remind us, that without His love, we are empty clanging vessels.

Yet when we stand with His love pouring from us, we can become the balm of healing that will revive the Church and prepare her for the Groom.

CHAPTER 15

SMASHING MUSICAL MINDSETS

Chapter 15 – Smashing Musical Mindsets

Does God like rock 'n' roll? I already touched on a bit of my testimony with regards to music, but I want to open the door a bit more and show you around.

You see, when I met my husband, I was not serving the Lord. Instead, I was a typical pastor's kid in a phase of rebellion. With my usual "all or nothing" kind of attitude, I was all "out there." If I could possibly find anyone or anything further from what a pastor should be, then that is what I was looking for.

I had vowed as a teenager that I would never marry a pastor. After a pretty tough upbringing, I blamed being a Christian for all the tough times. It was a short but very strong phase in my life where I decided, "That's it Lord, things have to be better than this."

I was in the middle of this personal discovery when I met Craig. He was so cool and he had everything that was completely opposite to anything that looked like a pastor. He was long-haired and deeply entrenched into the metal head culture.

He dressed like a typical metal head and acted like a typical metal head. I loved it. He was a typical rebellious type, and we would go to clubs and head bang together.

My parents thought, "Oh Lord, our daughter is lost!" and they were praying hard for me, that I would come back to the Lord.

GOD INTERFERES

My father shared the story with me, "One day we were praying and said to the Lord, 'You know what Lord, we are getting nowhere with Colette, so I am going to pray for this Craig guy she is with.'"

When he said that, he felt such a strong anointing that they looked at each other and said, "Okay, this is where we need to put our emphasis. This is what we are going to pray."

So from then onward, they stopped praying for me, and started praying for Craig.

Of course Craig had this weakness for music. It was his passion. In fact, when we were dating I always joked and said, "I come a close second to your music." He had a collection of everything.

He had built up a collection of heavy rock and metal music for years. He said music was his god. When he was down it lifted him up, when he was up it brought him down. That's the way it was.

So the Lord really showed me His sense of humor when He showed up and used the very vice the enemy had used to ensnare Craig - to win him for Christ!

One evening my parents invited us for dinner. So we accepted and as the Lord would have it, the evening found me helping my stepmom out in the kitchen, leaving Craig with my Dad.

Music Strikes Again

I heard my dad pick up the guitar. He was just playing some of his songs. I carried on and didn't pay any attention.

By the time we finished dinner and came through, Craig was on his face before the Lord."

I could not believe it! "I leave you alone for just a short time and look at what happens?"

I was so taken by surprise. In the middle of my whole rebellion and trying to run away from God, He goes and gets this guy, who I was falling in love with, saved.

Now I was really in a predicament.

The Prophetic Word

As if to make a point, the Lord did not stop there. My father laid hands on us and he gave us a prophetic word. He said that he saw us travelling on a plane, with two small children. He said we were going to go in the ministry, and we were going to go overseas.

That was a lot to chew on. Little did I know, that two years later, the vision would come to pass. That is a story itself - but what a transition Craig went through.

In a short moment he went from being an unbeliever, to getting born again. From there he got spirit-filled, moved to speaking with diverse tongues, prophesying, and hearing from God for himself.

But then came the crunch... it was time to let go of the music.

It was one thing to be born-again, but another to let go of his music... it had been his life. If you know anybody that is deep into the metal head culture, you will understand what a hold it has on them.

Making the Transition

I must say, my dad really understood. He didn't condemn Craig. Instead of trying to dissuade him, one of the first trips they went on together, was to a bookshop where they looked for some Christian heavy metal.

It probably wasn't the most anointed stuff, and it wasn't the best, but it started Craig on a journey that displaced the hold that music had on his life.

He was still a baby Christian and still learning, but it was a good transition for him. It helped him go from where he was, to where God wanted him to be. It was his first step in the right direction.

God had to use his musical templates. God had to use his musical likes to get him on the right track.

Understanding Musical Archetypes

Perhaps I have just shared Craig's story with you, but take a look at your life. See what music you listen to and you will realize that you have musical templates as well.

When it comes to ministry and especially the prophetic ministry - you can't get stuck in a musical archetype.

This is a problem in the Church. Music plays an important part of what you feel will help you enter into the anointing, depending on where you fellowship. Instead of music being something that unites the Church, musical archetypes separate the Church instead.

The Influence of Music

My father picked up his guitar, and through music, he reached Craig using the one thing that was the most special in his life. It is powerful. Just look at the things that people buy most often. From your music players to MP3s —music is everywhere. It is a huge industry, because music is a part of us humans. It is another characteristic to what makes us different from animals.

If you want to reach the Church, this tool will reach it quicker than any fantastic prophetic word or any words of judgment you can bring.

Music reaches us on a much deeper level. It goes past our intellect and understanding. It reaches us in our heart and our soul. It stirs up the emotions from the past.

There is this one store that we go shopping at. They always play 60's music, and it always puts me in a good mood because I have good memories of that kind of music. It triggers a certain era of my life. If they play it, it gives me good feelings - even though it is not Christian music.

I am not saying it is anointed. That's a something else altogether. No, God cannot anoint worldly music. Let's not go there.

> **KEY PRINCIPLE**
>
> A worldly song moves you because music creates emotion.

USING MUSICAL STYLES

When you are playing a style of music that other people like, their hearts open automatically.

Now you add the anointing to that and you will bring about a transformation to the body of Christ.

It is not going to happen while you are stuck in your musical mindsets though. That is what I have come to call to death in you, in this chapter.

Reaching Musical Templates

You must reach others using their templates - not by your own.

"Well, that's the music I like - it is the way I am."

Then change!

I don't care if you like folk music, rock music, or yodeling. I don't care if you like Mariachi music. That's great... but can you reach the Church with it?

You say, "Uh, I hate Mariachi music," but is there a Spanish church that might like that music, and could be reached with it? Then you better learn it, don't you think?

Defining Musical Archetypes

Variety is the spice of life. This is even truer when it comes to music! You get many who are like "musical foodies" – one flavor just won't do! Rather, they like to immerse themselves in many different styles.

If you are one of these, then you are well on your way to breaking free of the prison that threatens to lock up the anointing inside of you! While different musical styles are fun, we need to look a little deeper.

When someone becomes hooked onto a particular style, they latch on to a lot more than just the natural rhythm of salsa or country music. They embrace the culture of it. This is what I call a musical archetype.

We already spoke about how satan is a master musician, so it is no surprise that he would use this powerful force to keep us stuck in just one mindset. Clinging to one style of music goes a lot deeper than a personal preference. Doing so adheres you to a particular culture.

The Culture of Music

Just look around you to notice it. An 80's metal head could be seen from a mile away, sporting doc martins and long hair. Into Reggae? I can tell from the dreadlocks! A love of music turns into a bondage. When that happens, the enemy has something to control you with.

People start to cling to their own musical clique.

Soon, it is not about music anymore, but it is about the acceptance of an archetype. We see this in the world, but are we any different in the Church?

Just playing drums at a Baptist church showed me how strong of a bondage this is in church. In their minds - God could surely not anoint such a style of music!

Walk past a church during praise and worship and you can tell what their ethnicity is and what their doctrine is! Now while that is fine for every believer, it is not all right for you!

You need to be able to reach every person, tribe, and tongue! How can you do that when you imprison yourself within a musical archetype?

IDENTIFYING YOUR MUSIC TEMPLATES

Now I am laboring the point here because this is one of the deaths that you are going to face in your prophetic training. You have to learn to let it go. You have to be able to listen to music of all styles, and sense whether it is anointed or not.

I get people who say to me,

"I was walking along and suddenly they played a song on the radio. It was a worldly song, but I just felt the presence of the Lord. I felt goose-bumps all over! The Lord anointed it!"

No, the Lord didn't anoint anything! That is your template talking. Those are your memories of the past talking.

THE LORD CANNOT ANOINT WORLDLY MUSIC

You probably find that the song took them right back to an era in their lives that was good.

Haven't you noticed how some songs can make you depressed and some songs can make you happy? Just because your emotions are moved, you cannot say that it is anointed.

There are Christians walking around, listening to worldly music because they think that God can anoint worldly music. That is like saying, that God can anoint satanic rituals. God can anoint the Mormon Bible. God can anoint the Jehovah's Witness Bible.

No, He cannot anoint what is specifically used to serve the enemy.

HE CAN AND WILL ANOINT YOU

However, He can anoint you, so that you can release music that is anointed! The anointing comes from within our spirits. So if we don't have the anointing within us in the first place, how can we release anointed music?

That's why an unbeliever cannot release anointed music. They don't have the anointing of God within them.

Their own spirit contaminates what they release. What they release is contaminated from what they got from the enemy - not by what they got from God.

It reminds me of the time when the Philistines captured the ark and put it in the temple of Dagon. What happened? Did God anoint Dagon? No, He made Dagon fall flat on his face before Him. That is how God deals with the enemy. He destroys it. He doesn't anoint it and add to it.

I do not prescribe to that teaching and you won't even hear me refer to it because I think it is heresy. How can God anoint what was never submitted to Him in the first place? Only believers have the authority to anoint, because they have the Holy Spirit within them.

Archetype Based on Country

If you want to anoint music, and if you want to bring change to the Church, it is not going to happen with your little archetype and your little structure. Whether you are African American, South African, Swiss, Indian, or Mexican - you have your musical archetypes.

I have seen it. The most archetypes that I have ever seen in my life have been in the United States. There is one for everyone and then some. I never liked gospel music. I grew up disliking it, but you know what? Being in America, it turns out that it is a huge industry and that a lot of churches like that music. I had to learn to change my singing style.

You Have To Change To Reach People

The anointing is the same, but the style changes. If I am going to reach people, I have to change. It is not them that are the problem. Rather it is you, that is the problem.

"I went to a church and they didn't like my music…"

Then change your music. Don't expect people to change for you. Rather you change for them.

If you want the anointing of God to come, and if you want to bring change to the body of Christ, you have to change first.

When you let go of your templates, it will bring you into a new relationship with Jesus. It will bring healing. It will bring change, and a new life to you.

You will no longer be imprisoned and stuck in a little rut anymore. You will have a whole variety of music to tap into.

Maybe it is just because I am an expressive, but I love variety. I love change. I love to sing in different styles. I love to listen to music of different styles. It brings such freedom.

ARCHETYPE BASED ON PROGRAMMING

The problem is, you don't know that you are being bound. You just say,

"I like this kind of music." Do you really?

"It is just my taste." No, it is not your taste, but it is what has been programmed into you.

It is what you grew up listening to, and that's why you like that kind of music.

"Oh, it is just the music I like." No, it is not just the music you like - it is the music that you were exposed to. It is very likely the kind of music that your parents or your friends listened to. So you have come to love it because of the experiences around the music. It is all you know. That's why you love it.

BREAK THE BOUNDARIES

Come on - let's break the boundaries here. If you have never heard Christian rock or country, I have a challenge for you - go and find some. If you can't bear listening to Christian gospel, then go and find some!

What have you never listened to?

Yes, every musical style can be anointed. Does it mean that it is always anointed? Hardly! I have listened to typical praise and worship music that was so oppressed I had to turn it off.

Many believe that a certain style of music is more anointed than others. They say:

"Uh, it gives me goosies." Yes, it gives you goosies because it is your template. It is what you know, but it doesn't mean that it is anointed.

REACHING PEOPLE WHERE THEY ARE AT

You have to learn to differentiate from your archetype, your templates, and the real anointing. When you can learn that, you have a whole world that will open up to you. You can reach any person, at any time.

How much pressure are you putting on others, imposing your musical style on them? I don't care whether it is anointed or not. Maybe you can sense the anointing, but many people out there can't. If you come with a loud noise, whether it is anointed or not, they will run away. If it is music they don't like, they are not going to have their hearts open long enough to sense the presence of God.

> **KEY PRINCIPLE**
>
> You are called to initiate, so you are called to change. Take up the challenge.

Rise up in the anointing. Then release it through music with the authority of a prophet!

CHAPTER 16

LEADING WORSHIP LIKE A PROPHET!

Chapter 16 – Leading Worship Like a Prophet!

We have spoken a bit on music and how exciting it is. We have also covered how to tap into the anointing. Each principle has been borne out of experience. The Lord taught us how to reach the Throne Room by worshipping in the spirit. It was a season where we lived in the realm of the spirit.

I could not wait for the whole church to have this experience! With high ambitions, and armed with my usual prophetic passion, I hit the wall hard at one of our first public, prophetic conferences.

We were so used to getting into the presence of the Lord as a team. We would worship unashamed and unaware of anyone else in the room. Each one of us, tapped into the anointing for ourselves. There was never a leader. We tapped into the anointing individually, and in that, found our unity.

We experienced so many wonderful things in the Lord's presence. We imagined how natural it would be to have an international conference and how touched everybody would be with our praise and worship.

What a crushing reality it was when we faced a stone cold wall pressed up against our faces!

A Truth to Remember

It was devastating. The meeting started and we did what we usually did when we worshipped for hours in the secret of our room. We closed our eyes and in an instant we were in the Throne Room.

Then we opened our eyes. Everybody was staring right back at us.

> **Key Principle**
>
> People need to be taught how to enter into the presence of the Lord through worship.

We were stumped. This was not just any seminar either – it was a prophetic seminar! In our minds, they should have been able to sense the presence of the Lord – right?

It was then that we learned that entering into the presence of the Lord through worship is not natural. Not everybody knows how to get into the presence of the Lord.

When you stand up to lead worship - they wait for you to lead them into worship! We assumed that everybody would just know how to worship, feel the anointing, and enter in.

It didn't happen. They could feel the anointing and they could see that we were having a great time. They just didn't know how to have a great time with us.

We were both frustrated and discouraged. And so began my learning curve for releasing the anointing through praise and worship.

The Lord began to teach me how to lead others into experiencing the anointing for themselves, instead of always feeling as if they had to "hijack" someone else's time with the Lord.

The lesson is, just because you are able to enter the presence of the Lord easily through worship, does not mean everyone else does as well. It is so typical of us, as prophets, to get so excited about what is going on in the realm of the spirit, that we run with all passion towards the arms of Jesus – only to turn around and find everyone else staring at us with looks of skepticism.

THE INTERNAL ANOINTING

So far, I have been teaching you how to get into His presence and how to worship Him. That's fantastic. It is time though to learn how to take others by the hand and lead them there as well.

Just because you feel the anointing, see visions, and you are there, doesn't mean that other people are sharing your experience.

EXTERNAL VS. INTERNAL ANOINTING

When an evangelist stands up, they release the anointing, and it comes on God's people from without. In fact, that evangelist might not even feel that anointing. He will sure see the effects of it though!

The external anointing does not depend on you to pour it out. Rather it depends on you to stand in faith, and to ask the Holy Spirit to move.

Now for the reality check – you are a prophet! You flow in the internal anointing. That means that the Holy Spirit is going to be released as you pour out. The anointing is going to come from within.

Before you can release that anointing of course, it stands to reason that you fill up on Him first!

TAKE THE PEOPLE WITH YOU

If your focus is on Jesus, you will be filled up and you will feel the anointing empowering you. Once you have experienced that though, how about passing it on to the people?

You see, there was nothing wrong with us entering into praise and filling up on the Lord, but we did not stop long enough to take the people with us. We needed to invite them to experience that anointing also.

Like Miriam of old, we needed to sing, and invite them to follow along, as we did. We need not have "shut ourselves" away, but rather to have kept the door open for them.

How to Lead People Into the Presence of the Lord

So the million-dollar question - how are you going to do that? I am going to give you a couple of simple steps and then let's take it from there.

Step 1: Experience the Lord for Yourself

First, you have to learn to experience the Lord for yourself. Once you are in His presence, you can take other people to meet Him.

Pretty natural isn't it? Once you know somebody, you can introduce Him to others. That is why I love giving my prophetic students so many practical projects – especially those that lead them into His arms.

You see, it is not enough to know that you have the anointing. You have to learn how to experience the anointing for yourself in your private time.

You don't come to the meeting hoping that the anointing will just "be there." You should go to the meeting expecting the anointing to be there, because you have already tapped into it in your private time.

> **KEY PRINCIPLE**
>
> You should stand up to lead worship, expecting the anointing to be there.

It is like I taught you about the internal anointing. This isn't "Well, God will anoint or He won't."

No, you can tap into this anointing at any time, and you should go to a meeting already charged up.

The biggest mistake that you can make, is to think that you will get there and coast on the corporate anointing! If you didn't arrive with the anointing, you are not going to find it halfway through praise and worship. You better be filled already and geared up before you go.

You are headed for disappointment if you think that you will be leading worship at some random meeting, and suddenly, the anointing will fall upon you. It doesn't work that way for a prophet. Let it go right now.

STEP 2: SPEND TIME WORSHIPPING IN THE SPIRIT AS A TEAM

Learn to get into His presence on your own first. Learn to feel the anointing, and if you are a worship leader and work with your band, do it like we did.

Spend hours just worshipping in the spirit. Worship in tongues, sensing the flow and getting to hear the heartbeat of God. Learn to feel His gentle breeze and sense when you should speed up or slow down.

Learn to hear the heartbeat of God. When it comes to the public meeting, it is not time to suddenly start getting revelation and to say, "I need to get my spirit right with God."

You should come already filled with power and with your heart full of the spirit of God, so that you can impart it to the others and lead them.

Where do you have to lead them to, if you are not already on the mountaintop yourself? You have to lead them to the mountaintop.

So get yourself into the presence of the Lord, and get charged up. Then, when you are charged up, you can lead them and charge them up as well.

STEP 3: WARM UP DURING THE FIRST FEW SONGS

How do we do this practically? You come into the meeting. It has been a busy day, and perhaps you even faced some stress getting there.

Especially if it is a conference! Of course you had stress getting there, because that's always what happens with conferences! The unexpected always happens when you need it the least.

Moving on... you get into the presence of the Lord and you are thinking, "Lord I do not feel very anointed right now! I am still trying to repent for losing my temper at the driver that nearly ran me off the road!"

> **KEY PRINCIPLE**
>
> When leading worship, it is okay for the first song or two to chill out and to get into His presence. It is all right to take the time to say, "Okay, Lord, I need you here. Please help me out."

So take a few songs to say, "Lord, I submit myself to you." Get that lifeline hooked up.

Here is a point to remember - don't expect too much from the people just yet. They are warming up and you are warming up. Just get into His presence. Learn to sense His presence and feel that familiar flow.

Get your spirit, soul, and body focused on Jesus so that you can hear His thoughts and feel His heartbeat.

STEP 4: TRIGGER THOSE TEMPLATES!

I did not realize, when I first started out, how sensitive I had become to the realm of the spirit. Because I was worshipping in tongues so much, just two strums of the guitar, and I felt the Lord!

When it comes to a public meeting though, the people weren't already in the spirit, so they didn't feel the anointing at all. So even though you might love diving right into singing in the spirit, give everyone else time to catch up first!

Start out by singing something that is familiar to them. Sing a song that they like and that they can follow along with.

START WITH THE FAMILIAR

Remember what I shared with you about musical templates? This is where you use the principles you learned there.

> **KEY PRINCIPLE**
>
> When leading worship, start with the known and then take them to the unknown.

So start with singing in English (or their native tongue). Do this so that they start getting good and "happy feelings."

Once they have these "happy feelings," they will begin to open up their hearts. That's why in most churches, you start with fast songs first. Why? So that people can chill out a bit and start feeling good.

Remember - we are made of spirit, soul, and body, not just of spirit. So start with songs that are fun and lively. It helps everyone to lower their guard a bit.

STEP 5: BRING IT!

Once the walls are down, and you have their attention, now is the time to bring the anointing.

You get into the spirit, and keep going until you sense the direction the Lord wants you to take. You can even close your eyes and praise Him. Once you praise Him, and feel His presence, then you open your eyes and you release it.

> *KEY PRINCIPLE*
>
> The worst thing you can do is lead praise and worship with closed eyes from beginning to end.

People are following you. I don't follow a leader that closes His eyes while he climbs a mountain. I know, when we worship Him, we close our eyes and that's great, but if you are trying to lead the people into His presence, take all that anointing that you just received from the Lord and look at the people.

You begin by setting your eyes on Jesus until He is all you see. Then, turn your sight to His people, and give them all you have. See their needs and feel the heart of

God for them. When you sing a song, minister to them with that song.

When I am preaching, I don't preach with my eyes closed. I don't preach looking at the ceiling - I preach to the people.

When I am talking, I talk to the people and I touch their hearts. I am thinking about the people when I am talking – not myself.

I have done more teaching on how to lead worship in *The Minister's Handbook*, but if you can take these key principles, you will take your music ministry to new heights.

Worship is for the Church

There is a reason why the Lord has challenged you to appreciate different kinds of music. Not only do we, as prophets, help people to find their place in the Church, but we are also responsible to lead them into the presence of the Lord Jesus.

It is for us to teach them how to worship and be filled up. So when you stand up as a prophetic leader in the Church, it is not about what you do or do not like. It is not about how you prefer to worship, or what songs you like to sing.

It is about what the Lord wants His people to hear. It is also about what will reach His people. Start with what they know. Do not condemn their musical templates, but rather challenge your own.

The Lord has given you a heart to worship. It is not a heart that cares for talent, or cares much for being a superstar. You have in you the fire to make a real difference in the Church. This passion is from the Lord, prophet of God. Go that extra mile and let the Holy Spirit add even more to you!

Then stand up, see the needs of His people and unleash all that passion over them. After that... well... watch as God moves!

CHAPTER 17

THE PROPHET: ANOINTED TO WORSHIP

Chapter 17 – The Prophet: Anointed to Worship

For one called to be a prophet, the Lord sure chose an awkward place to start off my worship-leading career (albeit one of the most short-lived of my life!)

I had just started to learn how to play drums, and had started getting comfortable with myself as I reached to play the drums that were quite a distance above my small 12-year-old frame.

We had been attending a Baptist Church just down the road from our house. Now you must understand, this was a rather dramatic change of circumstances for us. My father was born during the early Pentecostal revival.

His mother was belting out tongues as she birthed him into this world. Demons, worship, tongues, and spontaneous worship was our spiritual "normal." We were a family of Charismatics born from a family of Charismatics.

Loud, proud, excessive, and yes…. playing drums. That was who we were… sitting, in none other than a very strict, religious Baptist church.

Who says that the Lord does not have a sense of humor? As the pastor and his wife came to know our family, they found out that we had our own little family worship band. My mother sang, my father played guitar and I accompanied them on the drums.

"Bringing It" to the Baptists

They invited us to bring our musical instruments and lead worship one Sunday morning meeting. We were so excited. We thought, "This is it! We are going to bring revival to this Baptist Church! Step aside tradition! Step aside songbooks! We were going to show these people what real worship was meant to sound like!"

Silence hung in the air as we strummed our last string. The meeting ended, our instruments were quickly packed up and most of the congregation avoided us after the service.

We were not asked to play again.

What happened here? We felt the anointing! We knew God showed up! However, short of just a few in the congregation that could sense God for themselves, everyone else was quite offended.

"God cannot be in such loud music!"

"It is sinful to use such contemporary music in the Church – that music is of the devil!"

Were they more worried about tradition than about what God was doing? Yes.

Were their hearts closed off to the anointing just because of a music style? Yes.

Was there an oppressive religious heaviness? You bet your socks, there was!

None of this was the point though. The point was, the worship we did was all focused on what we were going to bring to the people. Not once did we try to reach them where they were.

Had we given them something they were familiar with, their hearts would have been open enough for the Holy Spirit to touch them.

BRICK WALL OR OPEN HEART?

Instead of facing a spiritual brick wall, they would have been happy to hear what God had to say. It would have opened the way for us to introduce something later on. It could have been just what God wanted, to allow us to minister prophetically later on.

Unfortunately, the electric guitar and heavy bass drumbeat, killed any chances we could have had to minister what God really intended. The people could not find it in their hearts to look past the offense long enough, to see God behind it all.

Our focus should have been more on loving His people, than trying to prove a point. It was a lesson I will never forget. Although I still find in myself a small arrogance that really wants to worship "my way," I have learned, as Apostle Paul said, "... to the gentiles I became a gentile. I became all things to all men, so that I might win some!"

THE ANOINTING NEEDS FOCUS

I taught in *Hope – the Power of Focus,* that the Lord will give us the anointing and wisdom we need according to what we are focused on.

Depending on what we pray for, or on which promise we focus on, that will dictate what wisdom we receive.

It is a spiritual principle that I cover in that teaching in more detail if you want to get into the nitty-gritty of it.

Now if you let this principle sink in, you will realize how often you "waste" the anointing. How often are you focused on your insecurity or fears? How often have you allowed yourself to become distracted in praise and worship?

You fill your mind and thoughts with things that have nothing to do with Jesus or the needs of His people. So you lack the anointing. The anointing needs focus! What are you focused on?

> **KEY PRINCIPLE**
>
> When you begin by focusing on Jesus, you release everything you are to Him. In return, He releases right back to you and fills you up. That is the time to give the anointing within you a new focus!

Focus it on the needs of God's people.

LOOK AT THE PEOPLE'S NEEDS

First you praise the Lord and you say, "Lord, I love you. I make myself available." Then you think of the people. Look at them and say, "Lord, what are their needs? How can I minister to them?"

That is why most of the songs that we write have the emphasis they do - they are ministry songs. When I sing a song, I am thinking of the person that it touches.

When I am singing a song that I wrote with the lyrics, "I fell in love with Jesus…" I am not singing about my experiences. Rather, I am singing, "Lord, let them fall in love with you." As I sing, I am looking at each one with the cry in my heart, "You need to fall in love with Jesus." From there a heart of compassion easily flows.

As you have that outward focus and start looking at the needs of the people, you will see what is inside of them. From there, the Holy Spirit will give you what you need to meet those needs.

DON'T TRY IT IN YOUR OWN STRENGTH

An experience comes to mind, of a meeting where I was asked to preach. When we host our own meetings, we always do our own praise and worship. However, this time, we were traveling out, so the Church had a worship band.

The band took the stage and began trying to "drum up" the anointing. They were trying so hard. They were singing with all their heart and praying with all their might.

There was a long string of "glory hallelujahs" accompanied with many ardent "holy, holy, holies."

It all looked like quite an effort. My heart went out to them. I thought, "They are trying so hard, thinking that they had to perform to try and get God to attend the meeting."

Song after song continued with, "Come Lord, come Lord. Come Lord."

All the while I am hearing the Lord saying in the spirit, "I am here, I am here. People! I am here!"

They were trying so hard with their praise and worship to reach Him. They didn't realize that He was already there, waiting to speak to them.

He was waiting to love them, but they thought that they had to impress Him first.

Having an "Other-Orientation"

It was heart breaking to watch. As I sat there, I used the time to listen to the Lord about what He wanted for His people. Once they finished, I just picked up my guitar and played a song before taking the pulpit to preach. (Whether land, sea, or air… I always have a guitar close at hand!)

Craig and I played one or two songs. He played the guitar and I sang.

I sang one of my favorites about just knowing the Lord. It was a song I had written during a time when I too, was reaching out to touch Jesus. I found that all along - He was reaching back to touch me.

I looked at the congregation, and as I sang, I thought, "He is here. Just reach out and touch Him."

As always, the tears began to flow and the anointing came. It was a simple song. I was not thinking about how well I was singing, but I was just thinking about how I could meet the needs of the people.

I was focused on how to use the Lord's anointing to get His message across so that He could meet their needs. What a stark contrast this was to the story I related earlier about the Baptist Church.

The Holy Spirit came with a sweet presence, and I could move on to share about how the Lord Jesus wanted to call each one of them into a face-to-face relationship with Him.

The tears began to fall. The Holy Spirit healed broken hearts. It did not take a big performance to minister - it just took a little bit of other-orientation.

THE SECRET

When you have that orientation, and love motivation, the anointing will always be there. This is the hidden secret, to releasing the anointing in praise and worship.

Yes, get your spirit right. Begin by getting yourself in line, but then open your eyes to the people around you and see their needs. Don't think, "What do they think of me? What should I sing? I sure hope my voice doesn't break in this song...."

WORSHIP – A TWO WAY STREET

Worship is a two-way street. On the one hand, you need to be sensitive to the Spirit. On the other, you need to be sensitive to the needs of the people. You put the two together and you have the anointing.

When you are sensitive to the spirit, and the Holy Spirit stops pouring out, you can also stop. That is why you need to make sure you are in the Spirit first.

There is nothing worse than bringing the beautiful presence of the Lord, and then going beyond what God intended and kill everything that you started with!

Sometimes as prophets, we can swing the pendulum and try so hard to meet every need that we forget to take heed when the Holy Spirit is telling us, "Stop! It is time to step down now!"

Boy, do we know how to flog a dead horse! Another conference experience – this time I was leading the worship.

How to Fall On Your Face in Style

As I led the people in praise and worship, the Holy Spirit just showed up! It was probably one of the most anointed meetings I had led up until that point. It felt good to stand in that glory cloud!

I looked at the people and saw their needs. There were so many and my heart reached out to each one. So I progressed from worshipping in the spirit to ministering prophetically.

The Lord was with me each step of the way. I saw more needs. I realized how much more work needed to be done. The anointing felt good and I was on cloud nine. It was only after the accompanying pianist stopped playing to go on a desperate bathroom break, that I realized I had gone for nearly 2 hours!

In fact, I had pretty much preached the entire sermon of the speaker! I suddenly "woke up" and realized that the Holy Spirit had stopped talking a long time ago – I was simply riding the wave of the anointing and the fantastic experience.

I tore down what I had built up. I was tired, the people were tired and the guest speaker was not terribly impressed. Sure, I could say that I was just being a "real prophet" and that everyone else needed to "get with the program" or, I could just admit the truth!

I had gone beyond what God intended. There is a time to step up, and then there is a time to step down. Once the Lord has done what He wants, let someone else take the stage. Let's be real with one another here – sometimes we prophets just like the sound of our own voices!

> **KEY PRINCIPLE**
>
> So often we feel that our revelation is the only one that counts. Another reality check – the Church is a Body and not just a hand.

Play your part and do it well. Bring the glory to God's people and then step aside. Allow the person that follows you to catch the swell of the wave you just started, so that they can see it through.

We are, after all, a team. A team of fivefold ministers that each have a place.

TIME TO STEP UP!

It is time now to take what you have learned and apply it. Over the last couple of chapters, I have challenged you. I have challenged you to let go of all musical mindsets.

I have challenged you to walk in His love, and to release the gentle breeze of Jesus.

Now, the next opportunity you have - release His anointing! You can do it. When you have learned to praise and worship in your private times, do that before the meeting.

If you have time, even do it in the building beforehand. Get in His presence and tap into His anointing. Feel the flow and hear His voice. Say, "Lord, what do you want for your people?"

Then, when you stand up to minister and you strum that guitar, you are going to feel His presence. Now it is time to look at the people's needs.

You will never have to say, "I hope the anointing will be there." You know what? I don't even care anymore because I just want to love God's people. When your heart is set on loving God's people, the anointing will always be there.

This principle applies to all kinds of ministry. Whether you are giving a prophetic word, preaching, worshipping, or counseling, it doesn't matter.

> **KEY PRINCIPLE**
>
> When you love God's people, He will give you what you need to love them with.

HOW TO RECEIVE A DOUBLE PORTION OF THE ANOINTING

Love is the foundation of our Christian walk. Whether you love God's people with your guitar, counsel, or with your preaching – it does not matter. See their needs, and then hunger to meet them. Let it become a consuming passion in you. Put yourself aside.

When you can do that, the Lord will give you a double portion of His anointing.

Stop seeking the anointing so hard, and rather start seeking to love God's people and God will give you that anointing to love them with.

That is the secret to increasing the anointing in your life. If the anointing has vanished and nothing is happening when you minister, it is not God that is the problem. It is not even your righteousness that is the problem. The problem is that you stopped loving God's people.

When you stop loving God's people, you are in a very dangerous place. That is why I challenged you on your mindsets, on being bitter, and on judging others. By doing those things, you chase the anointing away.

Get the Anointing Back!

If you want to see the anointing back in your ministry in a greater portion than ever before, this is the key! If you want power and authority, then there is only one way to do it, by dying to yourself, and pouring out to others.

Learn to release His anointing in praise and worship, and you will have it on tap anytime and anywhere, with terrific power.

CHAPTER 18

IDENTIFYING PROPHETIC MATURITY

Chapter 18 – Identifying Prophetic Maturity

If you have ever been to a children's playground, you will be familiar with one of the most popular pieces of equipment that gave me endless hours of fun as a child. Regardless of the fact that my short little legs dangled when a friend joined me, the seesaw was still a fun experience.

If my sisters and I ended up on a children's playground, we would fly off to that first. Each of us taking a side, we would play for hours, seeing how high we could jump into the sky. Being so short, it did not take much to make me feel like I was being hurtled into the air!

Everything was fun and games until a rather large kid came along. The "vertically and horizontally gifted" child would came along and sit opposite me on that seesaw.

Without fail, they would tip me so much that my little legs would dangle in the air. I would be holding on for dear life, not being able to get myself down again because I was just too light.

As I take you by the hand now, to enter into the Throne Room of God and make your way to maturity, this illustration fits perfectly.

GOD WORKING WITH MAN

If there is one thing that you will come to realize along this road, it is that working with the Lord is a bit like being on a seesaw. He is on the one side and you are on the other. It is going to take both of you to accomplish this call.

Some prophets have it a little backwards. They think, "God helps those who help themselves."

Then, on the other end we have those that say, "Everything is up to the Lord. It is all by His grace and will alone."

Those in the second camp say, "So we wait for our destiny. We wait for the call. Therefore, if we have the call, God will do everything."

The first camp, are the guys who don't want to wait for the call, so they go ahead and do it all themselves. They are like a big kid sitting on the one side of the seesaw, not giving the other guy a chance to play.

COME TO BALANCE

You need to come into balance and realize that walking out your prophetic call is learning to work with God.

> **KEY PRINCIPLE**
>
> Prophetic maturity is learning that your call is about God working with and through man to accomplish what He needs to in this earth. It isn't you doing it yourself, or you standing there waiting for God to do it all by Himself.

Considering that you need to know what God's part is and also what He requires of you to do, you need to come into His Throne Room and ask. How could you possibly teach others to get direction for their lives, if you have not learned to do it for yours yet?

So for this chapter, I am going to take you by the hand to help you to enter into the Throne Room for answers, and to know what the part is that God wants you to play.

Soon what sounds difficult and heavily laden with "principles" will become easy and even fun – just like playing on a seesaw!

GOD'S CHASING YOU

> *1 Peter 2:21 For to this you were called, because Christ also suffered for us, leaving us an example, that you should follow His steps:*

How are you going to enter into the Throne Room? I have given you some teaching, and I think that you already have an idea, but the first step is realizing that the Lord is in charge.

He is the one that is going to initiate. So He is going to make the first step.

Isn't that what He did on the day of your salvation? God sought you out and chose you for Himself. Even then, He did not stop. In fact, I would daresay that it was then, that the chase really began.

The first conviction that you got was that you were a child of God. The second was even more shocking – you were called to be a prophet!

You did not ask for that grace. You did not earn it, and you sure knew that you did not deserve it. No, it was the Lord that came and gave you some of His grace. Just like it says in the scripture above, you were called because of Jesus!

From there, it is for you to follow in His footsteps.

You cannot decide to be a prophet. You cannot decide to shape yourself. Rather, you can look to the author and the finisher of your faith and wait on Him to initiate!

Paul refers to the relationship we have with the Lord as a romantic one. Jesus is our Groom and we are His

Bride! It is always for the Groom to initiate – it is for the Bride to respond.

And so Jesus makes the first step. He calls you to the seesaw and says, "Come on, come play with me. Come climb on board."

He woos you and draws you into His presence. Now before you think that this is something that just happens at the time of receiving your call, let me assure you it is not.

Hearing The Call to the Throne Room

This is an experience that you will have again, and again. This is especially true if when you are involved in full time ministry. So often we get caught up in our last "Throne Room experience" that we forget we need to visit again, and again.

If you are sensitive to the Spirit, you will know what I am talking about. You will be running on your track of the last thing the Lord told you to do. As you are running that race with all diligence, you will start to feel a tugging deep inside.

You will feel a hunger start to bubble up from inside of you. You will find yourself sneaking away to have a moment alone of praise and worship. Without even thinking, you will notice that you are withdrawing from others, trying to snatch moments in your secret place.

Your heart will be thirsting for something that you cannot see. You will experience a deep dissatisfaction inside of yourself. When this happens, you can be sure that the Lord Jesus is nudging you and saying, "Come. Come my child, and enter my Throne Room. There is more that I must show you."

Once you are in the Throne Room, the Lord can give you what He needs you to have. The more time you spend there and the more you follow His instructions, the more you will grow up.

Again, just like in the passage I used at the beginning, all you need to do is follow in Jesus' footsteps! The more you do it, the more you will mature.

SIGNS OF PROPHETIC MATURITY

I know - that as a prophet you are probably like me... impatient! You want maturity, now! You want to walk in perfection, now! When it comes to maturity though, you will find that it is progressive.

You will come to one level of spiritual maturity, only to discover that there is yet another level to go to! It is the natural order of growing up. My eldest daughter thought she was such a "big girl" at 5 years old. At 11 she realized how far behind she was and could not wait to be a teenager... and so the cycle of life continues until the day we die!

There are some signs though, to identify the level of your maturity. When my daughter took her first steps unattended, it was a sign that she was getting big! The day we handed her over the keys to her first car, I knew yet another level of maturity had come... for us *both*!

The same is true of your prophetic call. So let me remove some of the mystery and help you identify exactly how far you are.

1. You Are no Longer Compelled to Act

It is a happy day when you don't feel pushed to minister or "do" anything for the Lord. You know that you are growing up, when you know how to relax, even in the midst of pressure.

When you come to this place, you are like Elisha saying, "Open the eyes of my servant so that he can see that there are more for us than there are against us."

In the moment Elisha prayed, his servant's eyes opened and he saw angels in the spirit (that had been there all along). Elisha was chilled out and he wasn't compelled to act. (2 Kings 6:17)

His servant, on the other hand, had not come to that place of rest yet. Instead of trusting in the Lord, he was saying, "Oh the enemy is coming. We must lock the doors!" He was compelled.

You see in this event, the difference between the servant and the master. You can easily compare the one who is mature with the one who isn't.

Further along, when the enemy came to take on Elisha, they got blinded for all their troubles. Elisha acted at the right time - in God's time. He was not compelled to act.

2. You Know His Voice

The second sign is that you do not "shoot in the dark" any longer. You do not shoot blindly, hoping that you didn't miss the mark.

You do not share a word of encouragement or revelation saying, "Well, I hope that word was of God."

You come to a point where you know the Lord's voice so well, that you are sure when you have heard Him or not. This is a sign that you will mature from glory to glory!

In fact, just when you are sure you know His voice, He will sweep you off your feet by showing you an aspect to His nature that you never knew before. Every step of the way will be done as you rest securely in His hand.

You will never lose the righteous fear of knowing that without the Lord, you have nothing to give His people. You will never get to the place where you do not stand up in fear and trembling, knowing that unless the Lord shows up, you are sunk!

However, when He does talk, you will hear the inflections in his voice and revel in the melody of his revelation.

The hours you have spent, lost in His presence and swept up in praise will be the wind beneath your wings. Every moment that His words flooded over you in the deepest moments of your travail, will be the very essence of what you minister to others.

Prophetic maturity is about knowing His voice. Not just a voice you learned through study. Not just a voice you understand. Rather, you will know His voice through experiences you have lived in many intimate times with Him.

A mature prophet is not just one that talks about Jesus as they stand up front. He is one that converses with Him and revels in His presence, when there is no one around to see it.

When you know Jesus like this, you will experience a peace that passes all understanding. You will have such peace deep within that you will not feel compelled to force any word He gives you to share.

This peace will stem from the fact that you know that the word you have to share is His, and that He will give the opportunity for you to share it.

Faith will follow naturally from peace. You will speak that word in faith, knowing it will come to pass.

Look at how far you have come. Where are you at right now?

> **KEY PRINCIPLE**
>
> Are you still aiming wildly, "hoping that you have heard from the Lord?" or are you sure that the word you spoke is an arrow that hit the mark?
>
> This force of faith will leave you knowing, that every word that goes into the earth that was sent of the Lord, will not return void.

3. YOU SPEAK OUT OF REST

Remember those early days when you first found out you were called to be a prophet? None of us ever forgets the first time we received a prophetic word to speak out!

I was as dramatic as the next prophet when the bomb first hit that, "I am called to be His spokesman!"

I was prophesying over everyone. I was so excited. I was prophesying and sharing visions with anybody I could lay my hands on. I was so excitable.

Okay, maybe I am still a tad too excitable at times! That hasn't changed, but one thing I have learned, is to speak in rest. This is so important to help people feel at ease.

You know those nervous people, who always seem to get excited over everything? They can barely stand still and as much as they hop around, their mouth seems to follow suit?

You can't have a conversation with them for five minutes before you want to run out the door, because it is too intense.

You can't handle it because they are all hyped up or all cast down. There is no in between with them. You battle to take them seriously. You think to yourself, "How does this person make it in the real world?"

Don't laugh, because we both know that you were like that once! Hopefully you are not like that anymore. Hopefully you have come to a place where you can speak in rest.

Whether God gives you a word of judgment, encouragement, or warning - you say what needs to be said. You say it in faith, hope, and love, and then you know that your job is done.

Prophetic maturity has come, when flowing in the gifts is not so complicated anymore. Giving a prophetic word is not such a big deal and it is a rest.

When you speak for the Lord, you know that it has gone forth in power, and you know that you have done your job for that day.

4. You Speak in the Right Time

Your next sign of maturity, is that you speak at the right time. This is very important. We all get revelation. I get so many prophets contacting me. I don't know, maybe it is a prophetic arrogance, but so many think that they are the only ones that the Lord speaks to.

They get so caught up in their revelations that they think they are the only person in the world to get that single revelation!

It is not an easy pill, for prophets like them, to swallow when I say, "You know what guys? Everybody gets revelation. All prophets get revelation. In fact, God can speak to every believer. Even more shocking… God is even able to speak to the Pastor in the church you attend. You are not the only one who receives revelation."

> **Key Principle**
>
> The secret is not in getting the revelation. The secret to prophetic maturity is saying it at the right time.

You can have five prophets in the room and the Lord may give all of them the revelation. It is not about the revelation - it is about how you share them, and the time in which you share them. That is what sets you apart.

Just look at your life, as an example. Look at the times when the Lord gave you a word of encouragement that just came at the right time. Had that word come when you were feeling good, or when something else was happening, you wouldn't have noticed it. It would have just passed you by.

However, you remember those well-placed words that struck your heart. I have been at a place so many times in my life where I have hit a wall. Times, when I felt so low and said, "Lord, are you even out there?"

In these times, the Lord will lead me to read or listen to something and it will hit me between the eyes. It was the right word at the right time. Moments like these are the most changing of our lives!

The right word at the right time can change a person's entire destiny in life. So do not concentrate on your revelations, but on speaking them in the right time.

Rather have one well-placed revelation, than twenty that you just blabber off any time you want. Then you will start having a real impact in people's lives, and then you will have a place of maturity.

5. You Have the Ability to Be Silent

The next point is one that I really like to look out for in prophets in training, because it is quite defining.

If you know as many prophets as I do, you know how impossible this point sounds! The ability to remain silent? Yes, it is possible!

I think that this is a tough one because prophets always have so much to say and they have so many opinions. They have so many revelations, that they cannot even share them all sometimes.

However, when you have come to a place of maturity, especially if you work with other prophets, it is good sometimes, to step back and let somebody else have a chance.

When you come to this place of maturity, you will not have any problem stepping back. It will be nothing to you, to let the younger prophets have a chance to get all excited, and to spit and spew, and get their little moment of glory.

When you have been on the road a bit, you look at new prophets in training and think, "Wow guys, you have got a long journey ahead of you."

You needed that phase to get to where you are right now - so let them have their moment. You know what I am talking about. You see someone receive the first conviction of their prophetic all.

They are a bit like the army recruits, the new guys that come in all full of zeal. They think that they are going to "get in there" and show everyone how great they are.

All the senior officers are looking at them thinking, "Give it a few weeks, guys. We will temper you, we will take that zeal and shape it."

When you come to a place of prophetic maturity, you are not afraid to be quiet and to step back. Let other people spew out all their prophetic words and their fluff, because when you stand up and speak, it is not fluff anymore. It comes from a place of rest and power.

6. You Do Not Feel Pressured to Minister

This is really another sign of prophetic maturity. Somebody comes to you, desperate for a prophetic word, and at the beginning you may feel compelled, under stress, and you think, "I have got to give a word!"

Or, you sit in a church meeting and you see the pastor looking at you, expecting you to give the word and you feel pressured to get a revelation. Unfortunately, a lot of the time, you jump up and share a word that was not led, or not in the right time. As a result, things fall around your feet.

When you have been on the road a little bit, you will not allow that kind of pressure to influence you. I will not allow anybody in this world to put a demand on me, to get a revelation, or to speak a word from God because they don't like what I have said.

> **KEY PRINCIPLE**
>
> I will not allow to be pressured into giving a prophetic word, because the word is not mine to give, but the Lord's.

More times than I can count, I have had people come to me for direction regarding their call. They will share their revelations and their thoughts and there is no doubt that they want me to say, "Yep! You are a prophet!" or "Yes! You are an apostle."

Yet it is clear that neither of these is what God has in mind for them. So I will tell them exactly what I see in the spirit, and what God says. They will fight and say, "Well then, why do I get visions? Why does God say certain things to me?"

Instead of getting flustered, I respond with a simple, "Do you want me to tell you what you want to hear or do you want me to tell you what God really says?"

Perhaps that seems a bit harsh, but I say it from a point of rest, because I do not need to feel pushed to say the right thing to stay popular. I am not here to be popular. I am here to help people identify their call. If they do not like the calling that God has given to them, then they can take it up with Him!

I am not going to lie and make things up, just so that they put a little something extra in the "Blessing Box" on their way out!

It is His gift and His anointing. He will manifest it to whom, and where, and how He wills. Do not tell me that I must prophesy. Do not tell me what I must decree. Do not tell me I must get a revelation right now.

I will not be pressured. I will speak when God tells me to speak. When I do, it is going forth in power, and in authority, and it will accomplish that for which it was sent.

That is prophetic maturity.

You know who you are. You know what God has put in you, and you do not need to accept being manipulated. You see, I don't care if I get rejected. I don't care if I lose my friends. I don't care if I lose a contact, just because I wouldn't get a prophetic word for them.

I have seen this go wrong so often in the Church. I saw this go so very badly in a church once. There was an influential businessman in the church that contributed the lion's share of their financial support.

He started a new business venture that he stated would be "a real blessing to the church if he succeeded." So he ordered the prophets to pray. "Get a revelation for me."

Because so much of his finances came into the church, the prophets felt, "We better get a revelation! We better pray. We better speak something forth." They ended up getting into things God did not intend.

His venture failed, and instead of looking at his own failure, he blamed the prophets for giving the wrong revelations, and he blamed God for letting him down.

> **KEY PRINCIPLE**
>
> When you have come to a place of prophetic maturity, you are not pressured anymore to get a word or a revelation. You speak what God wants you to say, when He wants you to say it and how He wants you to say it!

7. YOU DISCERN TRUE AND FALSE

This comes with the gift of discerning of spirits. When you are in a meeting and around people, you know what is of God and what is not of God. You know what is false and what is true.

Between your knowledge of the Word and the gift of discerning of spirits, you know what is right and what is wrong. You are not led by your emotions.

It is the same concept of what I shared regarding music. You can sense when something is anointed and when it is not. It is not just because it hits your emotional templates, but because you know the anointing by the gift of discerning of spirits.

This is another one of those signs that are progressive. This particular maturity is not one that you just reach one day and so remain there. Rather, it is one that you will delve deeper into as you continue your prophetic journey.

8. Face-to-Face Relationship With Jesus

This is probably the most profound point in my opinion and one I look for in every prophet that comes my way.

> **Key Principle**
>
> I can sum up all the signs of prophetic maturity with this statement:
>
> Prophetic maturity is found in the level of intimacy that the prophet has with Jesus.

Identifying Prophetic Maturity

When I see a prophet with a face-to-face relationship with Jesus, then I know I am with a prophet that is mature. Such a prophet knows how to get into the Throne Room and then to take what he hears there and imparts it to others.

If you are walking in prophetic maturity, then you are walking in a face-to-face relationship with the Lord. When this happens, the other signs become a lot easier to follow.

When you are in a face-to-face relationship with Jesus, you know when to sit down and shut up. When you are in that relationship, you know what is true and what is false.

When you know Him, you never feel pressured, because He doesn't pressure you. You don't feel compelled and you don't shoot in the dark.

You can speak in rest, and you speak in the right time because that is the foundation of your prophetic call.

STEP OVER THE THRESHOLD

Each lesson that you have learned in this book has led you to this point of maturity. The hours you have spent in worship have conditioned your soul. All the dying you did to "self" emptied you, so that all that remained was His anointing.

Sometimes it feels as if all we do is have ourselves emptied out! When you come to the place of realizing that there is a joy in that, you will be like the woman with the issue of blood, clinging to the hem of your Savior.

When you are hungry, He will feed you. When you are thirsty, He will fill you up with His living waters. When you allow yourself to be emptied, He will fill you up. The more you strive to be like Jesus, the more you will rise up in His authority.

Soon, you will stand, not in your templates and great ideas. Soon you will stand and reflect Jesus. Then the church will look at you and see hope. They will know that Jesus is not far away. They will feel His arms wrapped around them.

Prophet of God, this is our goal. To introduce a desperate church to the one that loves her. You have faced so much already! Yet there is more to come. You have learned in this book how to tap into His anointing.

What Lies Ahead

This is essential, because from here I am about to take your hand and lead you into the wilderness. Just as Jesus had to face his temptations and qualify for his call, so also does the wilderness stretch before you.

You do not need to be afraid though, because you have everything you need to face it. You have rivers of living water inside of you. You have the bread of life in your belly. You are ready.

I pray that you leave this last page, armed with His anointing. You will need it now as you step across the threshold of the next phase of your journey – prophetic training!

Do not worry though, because I will not leave you hanging. Join me in my next book, *Prophetic Boot Camp* as I take you through that wilderness. By the end of it, not only would you have mastered this season of training, but finally hold in your hand, the office of prophet.

About the Author

Born in Bulawayo, Zimbabwe and raised in South Africa, Colette had a zeal to serve the Lord from a young age. Coming from a long line of Christian leaders and having grown up as a pastor's kid she is no stranger to the realities of ministry. Despite having to endure many hardships such as her parent's divorce, rejection, and poverty, she continues to follow after the Lord passionately. Overcoming these obstacles early in her life has built a foundation of compassion and desire to help others gain victory in their lives.

Since then, the Lord has led Colette, with her husband Craig Toach, to establish *Apostolic Movement International,* a ministry to train and minister to Christian leaders all over the world, where they share all the wisdom that the Lord has given them through each and every time they chose to walk through the refining fire in their personal lives, as well as in ministry.

In addition, Colette is a fantastic cook, an amazing mom to not only her 4 natural children, but to her numerous spiritual children all over the world. Colette is also a renowned author, mentor, trainer and a woman that has great taste in shoes! The scripture to "be all things to all men" definitely applies here, and the Lord keeps adding to that list of things each and every day.

How does she do it all? Page through every book and teaching to experience the life of an apostle firsthand and get the insight into how the call of God can make every aspect of your life an incredible adventure.

Read more at www.colette-toach.com

Connect with Colette Toach on Facebook!
www.facebook.com/ColetteToach

RECOMMENDATIONS BY THE AUTHOR

If you enjoyed this book, we know you will also love the following books on the prophetic.

PROPHETIC BOOT CAMP

Book 4 of the Prophetic Field Guide Series

By Colette Toach

The way of the prophet is one that goes through the cross, surrenders in death and rises up in resurrection power and authority. Deep inside you know that you have not gone through this hard road just to come out defeated. You have paved the way for others.

For it is in the training of the prophet that he begins to realize that all of His scrapes and bruises along the way are the very thing that the people will be able to identify with.

So, prophet of God, are you ready to sign up for boot camp? The Holy Spirit will be your sergeant and this book will be your training manual! Together you will be shaped, challenged, inspired and in the end, equipped to stand as a prophet in office.

PROPHETIC WARFARE

Book 5 of the Prophetic Field Guide Series

By Colette Toach

A true warrior holds no excuses of why he cannot defeat his enemy and so is true with a genuine prophet of God. He is ready to take up the weapons of warfare that God has prepared for Him and to set the captive free and to heal the broken hearted.

Prophet of God, now is the time to face your own limitations and your own bondages and to see what has been holding you back from walking as the warrior that God has called you to be.

PROPHETIC FUNCTIONS

Book 2 of the Prophetic Field Guide Series

By Colette Toach

There is so much more to the prophet than standing up in church and prophesying.

Laid out beautifully so that you can understand and relate, Colette shares from her own personal experiences. Be prepared to live and experience the Lord like never before. This is not fiction... this is your training guide to the prophetic.

PRESENTATION OF PROPHECY

By Colette Toach

You do not need to be a prophet to prophecy and God will not come forcibly on you and make you do anything.

It is indeed a gift of the spirit that can be practiced. By the end of this book, you will be amazed to discover how accessible this gift of the Holy Spirit is to you. You will know the steps 1, 2, 3 of presenting prophecy.

PRACTICAL PROPHETIC MINISTRY

By Colette Toach

Wouldn't it be incredible if someone could have walked you through your prophetic calling and pointed out all the potholes before you fell into them?

Unfolded step by step, you will have someone along the way telling you what to avoid, what to embrace and most importantly... what to do next along your prophetic journey.

Practical Prophetic Ministry is your guide along this journey. Taking you through training and pointing out the way you need to go, it is a must if you have a prophetic calling.

A.M.I. Prophetic School

www.prophetic-school.com

Whether you are just starting out or have been along the way for some time, we all have questions.

Who better to answer them than another prophet!

With over 18 years of experience, the A.M.I. Prophetic School is the leader in the prophetic realm.

From dedicated lecturers to live streaming and graduation, the A.M.I. Prophetic School is your home away from home.

What Our Prophetic Training Accomplishes

Our extensive training is a full two-year curriculum that will:

1. Identify and confirm your prophetic call
2. Effectively train you to flow in all the gifts of the Spirit
3. Fulfill your purpose as a prophet in the local church
4. Take your hand through the prophetic training process
5. Specialist training in spiritual warfare
6. Arm you for intercession and decree
7. Minister in praise and worship
8. Achieve prophetic maturity

CONTACT INFORMATION

To check out our wide selection of materials, got to: www.ami-bookshop.com

Do you have any questions about any products?

Contact us at: +1 (760) 466 - 7679
(8am to 5pm California Time, Weekdays Only)

E-mail Address: admin@ami-bookshop.com

Postal Address:

>A.M.I
>5663 Balboa Ave #416
>San Diego, CA 92111, USA

Facebook Page:
http://www.facebook.com/ApostolicMovementInternational

YouTube Page:
https://www.youtube.com/c/ApostolicMovementInternational

Twitter Page: https://twitter.com/apmoveint

AMI Bookshop – It's not Just Knowledge, It's **Living Knowledge**

Colette Toach

www.ingramcontent.com/pod-product-compliance
Lightning Source LLC
Chambersburg PA
CBHW070638160426
43194CB00009B/1488